THE *Bluffer's®* GUIDE T

BE█R

D1148123

Jonathan Goodall

Colette House
52-55 Piccadilly
London W1J 0DX
United Kingdom

Email: info@bluffers.com
Website: bluffers.com
Twitter: @BluffersGuide

Published 2013
Copyright © Bluffer's® 2013

Publisher: Thomas Drewry
Publishing Director: Brooke McDonald

Series Editor: David Allsop
Design and Illustration: Jim Shannon

ISBN: 978-1-909365-52-0 (print)
      978-1-909365-53-7 (ePub)
      978-1-909365-54-4 (Kindle)

CONTENTS

'Beer, it's the best damn drink
in the world.'

Jack Nicholson

DON'T BE A BEER MUG

You cannot have failed to notice, even in dreary old supermarkets, that there's something afoot in the beer aisles. Raise your line of sight above the BOGOF (buy-one-get-one-free) packs of lager, depressingly cheaper than bottled water, and you will see bottles brimming with possibilities: beers flavoured with basil, watermelon or chestnut; ales aged in old whisky or cognac barrels; ales brewed by monks and fermented with wild yeast (Brettanomyces bruxellensis, no less). Nowadays, beer labels are singing the praises of hop varieties with names like music hall acts (Fuggle and Golding), and in Restaurant Le Posh you might even be presented with a 'beer list' by a young and happening 'somm-ale-ier'.

There are various drastic measures you could take to be mistaken for a beer expert. You could grow a beard, sport chunky knitwear, take up the bodhrán, or even steal a British Guild of Beer Writers' tie bearing its proud quill and tankard livery (you wouldn't want to double up the tie with the knitwear, obviously). Alternatively, you could breeze through this book.

It sets out to conduct you through the main danger zones encountered in beer discussions, and to equip you with a vocabulary and an evasive technique that will minimise the risk of being rumbled as a bluffer. It will give you a few easy-to-learn hints and methods designed to allow you to be accepted as a beer connoisseur of rare ability and experience. But it will do more. It will give you the tools to impress legions of marvelling listeners with your knowledge and insight – without anyone discovering that, before reading it, you didn't know your butt from your firkin (108 gallons versus 9 gallons, since you ask). Even as we speak, a thriving craft brewing scene is eroding the edifice of mass-produced, perma-chilled blandness as slowly but surely as meltwater trickling through a glacier. A brave new world of beer is stretching out before us – a veritable bluffer's paradise.

FROM BEER TO ETERNITY: A BRIEF BREWING HISTORY

9000 BC Year Beero? We can infer from crop patterns that the ancient Mesopotamians were no strangers to a cheeky beer. Thus, the cradle of brewing lies, somewhat ironically, in the heart of the Middle East.

7000 BC The guesstimated date of pottery fragments with telltale beer residue found in the Hunan province of China.

4000 BC The ancient Sumerians produce clay tablets depicting the brewing process. Historians claim this could be the world's oldest recipe. According to the tablets, drinking beer makes us feel 'exhilarated, wonderful and blissful'. Raise your glass to Ninkasi, Sumerian goddess of brewing.

3000 BC Egyptian brewers decide that barley is the best grain for brewing, and soon develop crude forms of malting. The ancient Egyptian hieroglyph for meal is 'beer + bread'. Meanwhile, stonemasons working on the pyramids are paid in 'kash', a primitive beer probably sweetened with dates, aniseed, honey and saffron.

2000 BC In Europe, the Celts are brewing with barley, wheat and oats.

200 AD The Babylonians start cultivating hops.

740 AD The Germans catch on, planting their own hop gardens in the Hallertau region of Bavaria.

1040 The Weihenstephan brewery, the world's oldest brewery still in production, is founded near Munich.

1086 The Domesday Book registers 43 commercial breweries operating in England.

c 1150 In the first written account of brewing with hops, Benedictine abbess Hildegard von Bingen, in the Rhineland, observes in her treatise, *Physica*, that hops are a worthy replacement for 'gruit', a mixture of herbs used to flavour and preserve beer. The abbess is also said to be the first person to write about the female orgasm.

1295 Good King Wenceslaus II looks out, and awards the right to brew to 260 grateful citizens in Pilsen, Bohemia (Czech Republic).

c 1400 Lager is born, though the dark, cloudy style is not as we would recognise it today. Central European brewers find they can create cleaner, crisper beers by brewing and storing them in cool caves. *Lagern* means 'to store' in German. Though they are yet to discover yeast, or identify its role in brewing, they stumble across the lager-making process of 'bottom fermenting' where fermentation is much colder and slower. Ales, of course, are 'top fermented' (*see* page 28).

c 1500 British brewers begin their love affair with the hop, once dismissed as 'a wicked and pernicious weed'. Most English beer is made at home by 'alewives', seeing as they use virtually the same ingredients (minus the hops) to make bread. The best alewives display long poles covered in evergreens and/or hops ('ale stakes') in their windows to attract custom, thus inventing pubs and pub signs.

1516 Duke Wilhelm IV of Bavaria draws up the Reinheitsgebot, the German beer purity law, decreeing that German beer must be made only from water, barley and hops (remember, no one's discovered yeast yet). What seems a grand gesture to protect the traditions of German beer-making is really a practical measure to prevent brewers from using wheat, which is more urgently needed to make bread.

c 1550 Europeans are drinking more beer than water. Beer is the safer option because its water content has been boiled. Queen Elizabeth I of England starts each day with a quart of beer; that's two pints on the royal cornflakes every morning.

1632 The Dutch West India Company opens the first commercial brewery in North America, in Lower Manhattan, New York. Buffalo, Brooklyn, Albany and Philadelphia become early brewing centres. Hop cultivation begins in the New World.

1698 Shepherd Neame, England's oldest surviving brewery, is established in Faversham, Kent.

1722 The Bell Brewhouse in Shoreditch, London, makes the first porter from dark-roasted barley. Tax on gin, 'mothers' ruin', is raised threefold because it's ruining too many mothers. Porter becomes 'the universal cordial of the populace'.

c 1750 Newfangled coke ovens, as opposed to wood or coal, allow English maltsters to avoid burning their malt for the first time. Pale malts make pale ales.

1759 Arthur Guinness buys a disused brewery in Dublin. The rest, appropriately, is history.

1777 The first steam engine is installed in a brewery, at Stratford-le-Bow, east of London.

1785 Joseph Bramah invents the beer handpump, changing the way beer is served in pubs.

c 1790 Pale ale mutates into a turbo-charged version called India Pale Ale (IPA), heavily hopped and high in alcohol to withstand the long sea voyage from England to India. Beer geeks still get their knickers in a twist over whether or not IPA was invented by George Hodgson of the Bow brewery in London.

1810 The first Oktoberfest, now the world's biggest beer party, is held in Munich to celebrate the marriage of Crown Prince Ludwig of Bavaria and Princess Therese of Saxony-Hildburghausen.

1817 Porter and stout get richer and darker thanks to Daniel Wheeler's patent roasting machine, a rotating drum similar to a coffee roaster allowing brewers to make dark and 'chocolate' malts without burning the barley.

1842 At last! Bavarian brewer Josef Groll creates the world's first golden lager in Pilsen, Bohemia. A lager landmark of epic significance, Groll's Pilsner style goes on to achieve global domination, accounting for some nine out of 10 beers consumed today. All lagers were dark until Groll blew the doors off.

1857 Eureka! Louis Pasteur unravels the mysteries of yeast, making the breakthrough we'd all been waiting for. He establishes that yeast is not, as is widely believed, a divine gift called 'God is good', but a single-celled microorganism (a fungus) that can be manipulated to the benefit of beer. In 1876 Pasteur cements his position as the father of modern brewing with the publication of his seminal brewers' troubleshooting guide *Etudes sur la Bière*. He blots his copybook, as far as 'real ale' campaigners are concerned, by inventing pasteurisation. It creates clean beer at the expense of flavour, they argue.

c 1875 Lager brewing goes ballistic thanks to refrigeration technology devised by German engineer Carl von Linde. Storing lager in cold caves is suddenly very passé. Gabriel Sedlmayr II at Munich's Spaten brewery is the first to brew golden lager on a massive scale.

1876 The Bass brewery in Burton upon Trent registers its iconic red triangle, Britain's first trademark. E Anheuser & Co launches Budweiser in the USA.

1883 Pasteur crosses the ball; Emil Christian Hansen heads it in. A scientist and part-time novelist working for Carlsberg in Copenhagen, Hansen discovers how to isolate and cultivate a single, pure strain of yeast – in this case, Saccharomyces carlsbergensis. This breakthrough allows brewers to cultivate and store their own specific yeast strains, consigning the 'suck-it-and-see' approach to the history books.

1892 William Painter of Baltimore, USA, patents the 'crown cork' (bottle cap), and a machine capable of sealing 100 bottles per minute.

Late 1800s Coinciding with railroads and refrigeration, the second wave of European settlers, from Germany and Bohemia, settle in North America. From breweries in Cincinnati, St Louis and Milwaukee, lager's assault on ale begins.

1904 In the USA, the Toledo Glass Company unleashes the first fully automatic bottle-making equipment. Bottling beer has never been so cheap, quick and easy.

1911 While touring Britain, Harry Houdini accepts a challenge from Tetley's brewery in Leeds to escape from a padlocked beer-filled churn. He is overcome by carbon dioxide and has to be rescued. (Waiter! There's an escapologist in my beer!)

1914-1918 The lights go out over Britain as killjoy Liberal politician and paramour, David Lloyd George, restricts licensing laws to boost the war effort. Adding insult to injury, great British beers are made to much weaker recipes; a cruel legacy from which we are only beginning to recover.

1920-1933 Prohibition, or 'the Noble Experiment', proves not so noble after all, creating perfect conditions for a tidal wave of organised violent crime across the USA.

'Beer is proof that God loves us and wants us to be happy.'

Benjamin Franklin (possibly)

1922 Shandy is 'invented'. Running short of beer, Bavarian landlord, Franz Xaver Kugler, becomes the first person to dilute it with lemonade. Sadly, his name does not come to be associated with his invention (unlike the Earl of Sandwich, for example).

1927 Colonel Porter creates Newcastle Brown Ale, which is ironic, considering his name. It wins first prize for bottled beer at London's International Brewers' Exhibition the following year.

1930 Watney's of London trials pasteurised keg beer; a move that will eventually inspire a backlash from the Campaign for Real Ale.

1939-1945 Heroic RAF aircrew coin the euphemism 'gone for a Burton' to replace the phrase 'missing in action'.

'Burton', of course, refers to beer from the famous brewing town of Burton upon Trent.

1935 Krueger's Finest from New Jersey is the first beer launched in a can. A device called a 'church key' is required to open it; a post-Prohibition dig at the temperance movement?

1963 British brewers begin to favour metal casks over barrels, prompting the formation of the Society for the Preservation of Beer from the Wood (SPBW). In the USA, pull tabs are introduced on metal beer cans.

1971 Drowning in an ocean of bland, filtered, pasteurised keg beers, a small band of diehard British ale drinkers forms CAMRA (Campaign for Real Ale). It originally stands for the Campaign for the Revitalisation of Ale until they coin the term 'real ale' to describe unfiltered, unpasteurised cask-conditioned beers.

1976 Inspired by these same British ales during his military service in Scotland, Jack McAuliffe establishes America's first microbrewery in Sonoma, northern California. It closes in 1982, but the torch has been lit for the American craft beer movement.

1977 Only 167 years after Munich's inaugural Oktoberfest, Alexandra Palace in London throws open its doors for the first Great British Beer Festival. With a great sense of timing, the late Michael Jackson (not the squeaky 'moonwalker') publishes his *The World Guide to Beer,* the bible for beer aficionados.

1978 Jimmy Carter signs into US law the right for Americans to home brew. Meanwhile, in the Beer Can Regatta, first staged in Darwin, Australia in 1974, the Can-Tiki, made from 15,000 'tinnies' makes it all the way to Singapore.

1982 Only five years after the first Great British Beer Festival, the first Great American Beer Festival is held in Boulder, Colorado.

1985 Beer drinkers take to wedging limes into their beer bottles, especially if the provenance of the beer is Spanish or South American. Nobody knows why, but it catches on.

1989 Quelle horreur! 'Euro-fizz' lager becomes the most widely drunk beer in Britain, knocking ale off its perch. The Beer Orders brings better news for ale drinkers, restricting the number of 'tied' pubs that can be owned by the big brewery groups and allowing the pubs' tenants to stock a guest ale of their choice.

2002 Chancellor Gordon Brown introduces Progressive Beer Duty (PBD) in Britain, which means that brewers pay tax according to their production. Consequently, the smallest producers pay only 50% of the standard duty rate, a huge boost for the fledgling microbrewing movement.

2004 Andy 'The Viking' Fordham wins the Lakeside World Darts Championship. He maintains his performance-enhancing, body-mass stabilising belly by drinking at least 15 bottles of beer before competing.

2008 The big get bigger as American brewing giant Anheuser-Busch merges with InBev (itself a merger of Interbrew of Belgium and AmBev of Brazil).

2012 The tide could be turning. The British brewing industry's annual Cask Report shows that pub-goers quaffed 633 million pints of real ale in 2011, slightly up on the previous year, as the grip of 'industrial' lagers begins to loosen.

To be continued…

WORTS AND ALL:
HOW BEER IS MADE

If you're going to hold court in The Royal Oak, recounting your adventures among the 'wild' lambic beers of Payottenland (read on), you'll need to know, at the very least, how beer is made. Such knowledge will defuse any awkward 'saloon-bar moments' when the music suddenly stops and everyone turns to stare at you with a mix of pity and suspicion. Armed with an understanding of the brewing process, you can stare down even the most persistent inquisitor with the cold-eyed, unflappable cool of a gnarled gunslinger.

Beer is made to an age-old formula; barley + yeast + water + hops = beer. Brewing beer uses similar ingredients to baking bread (bar the hops) but it's the finely judged tweaks and careful decision-making of skilled artisans that elevate a humble brew to heaven in a glass, something you might describe as 'beervana' (or perhaps not). Continuing with the bread analogy, there's a world of difference between sliced white and something weird called pumpernickel.

While winemakers can whinge about the vagaries of

the vintage or tainted corks, thus transferring the blame for a shoddy Chardonnay onto circumstances beyond their control, the buck stops with the brewer. Assuming the barley arrives in good condition, he has full control of the process and responsibility for the results. While winemakers have just grapes to work with, brewers manipulate different combinations of cereals, hop varieties, specific yeast strains and even different types of water to create a balanced brew. Colour, strength, sweetness, bitterness, aroma, even the tint and consistency of the head are for the brewer, not Mother Nature, to decide. What this boils down to is that the brewer has a much wider palate of flavours to play with than the winemaker.

The basis of brewing is to turn barley into malt, extract its sugars in a watery solution, boil it with hops and ferment it with yeast. The process starts with the three 'M's: malting, milling and mashing. It's easy to remember thanks to the alliteration; or just think 'Mmm, beer', like Homer Simpson.

First the malting part: the barley is encouraged to germinate (i.e., sprout) by steeping it in water. The grain converts its starch into sugars to fuel this process. Germination is stopped by heating the grains in a kiln, with the degree of roasting affecting the style of the finished beer. Next, the malt is milled (ground) into a fine mixture of flour and husks called 'grist', so that the sugars are more soluble in hot water. The mashing part involves mixing the grist with hot water in a vat called a 'mash tun', to make a sweet, sugary solution called 'wort' (you, of course, know that this is pronounced 'wurt' to rhyme with hurt). This is run off into a large copper container ('kettle') and brought to the boil, often with some hops thrown in.

When the wort has cooled, the hops are strained off and it is transferred into a large, open fermenting vessel. Yeast is added (or 'pitched in'), which consumes the sugar, producing alcohol and carbon dioxide in the process of fermentation. Ale is top-fermented, and lager is bottom-fermented (again, as we've discussed previously). After a few days, the fermentation is complete and the beer – for it is now beer – is filtered off into a maturation vessel. Ta-da!

Of course, how the beer is conditioned is of crucial importance, dividing beer drinkers into two camps, with happy quaffers on one hand, and real-ale aficionados on the other. Nitrokeg beers, for the happy quaffers, are filtered to remove any yeast sediment, pasteurised and pepped up with nitrogen. This makes for a clear, clean, fizzy beer, which real-ale fans would argue is devoid of flavour. Some snootily refer to them as 'veneer beers'. The big brewers and pub chains are generally happier to work with nitrokeg beers because of their substantially longer shelf life and often, quite puzzlingly, greater profitability.

'Real ale' is the name given to cask-conditioned beers. Neither filtered nor pasteurised, they leave the brewery in an unfinished state as they continue to mature via a secondary fermentation that takes place in the pub cellar. As they mature, they gain slightly in strength and complexity, rewarding those worthy publicans who can be bothered with careful cellar management.

Like cask-conditioned beers, bottle-conditioned beers also undergo a secondary fermentation, only in bottles. If your bottled beer contains sediment at the bottom, it's fair to assume it's bottle-conditioned; another clue would be the words 'bottle-conditioned' emblazoned on the label.

Good lagers (as opposed to 'fighting lagers') are cold-stored for at least a month – the longer, the better – to allow their authentic dry, crisp flavours to fully develop and integrate. Before refrigeration, lager-style beers were stored in cool caves so that they wouldn't spoil over the summer, and so the clean, refreshing style developed.

MAIN GRAINS

Barley is the cornerstone of most beers, but it is not the only grain used. The Belgians and Germans are dab hands at wheat beers, after all. But barley remains the brewer's first choice because it is easy to work with and comparatively rich in fermentable sugars, producing soft, sweetish flavours, best described as 'beer-like'. Wheat, you can point out, makes sharper, tarter tasting beers and, of course, is needed first and foremost to make bread.

Uniquely, barley maintains its husk during the malting process and this acts as a natural filter when the wort is separated from the spent grains. Corn, rice, rye and even wheat take longer to release their sugars, and break down into a soggy, pasta-like mulch that can clog up the mash tun. Refer to any cereal used in brewing, other than barley, as an 'adjunct'. This can include sugar syrup, which is sometimes used as a cheap substitute in industrial lager brands.

The use of corn and rice is largely limited to the USA and Australia where their neutral character can be relied upon to make high-volume, inoffensive beers. Quinoa and sorghum are used to make gluten-free beers, which, unfortunately, don't taste overly beer-like. In practice, many brewers supplement malted barley with various combinations of adjuncts, both malted and unmalted, according to the style of beer they're aiming for and, of course, their budget.

If you see 'two-row' or 'six-row' barley mentioned on a highfalutin label, it refers to the number of rows of kernels on the barley stem. Most brewers favour two-row barley, which is especially rich in starch – hence, fermentable sugars – and low in protein.

Having settled on the variety of grain they will use, maltsters (those who make malt) can create an enormous array of flavours according to the length of time and the temperature at which the grain is kilned. At one end of the spectrum, lightly roasted barley (sometimes known as white malt) gives light, biscuity flavours, while at the other end, heavily roasted dark and chocolate malts create both the body and the coffee and bitter chocolate flavours in porters and stouts. Unsurprisingly, medium-roasted malts, such as crystal malt, are favoured for medium-bodied ales, imparting caramel, toffee-like qualities. The degree of roasting of the malt will also affect the hue of the brew. Refer knowledgeably to the most extreme example of malt manipulation, where it is smoked over beechwood to create the acquired 'smoky bacon' taste of German rauchbier. Big in Franconia, don't you know?

Amaze your chums with the revelation that in 2008 Sapporo Breweries of Japan produced 100 litres of a beer called Space Barley, using barley that had been grown on the International Space Station. We're sure it tasted out of this world, albeit lacking in (original) gravity.

HIP HOPS

Grains are to beer what grapes are to wine – the source of fermentable sugar, but there's something not very sexy about a sack of barley. Instead, beer labels are increasingly drawing our attention to hop varieties, naming the likes of Saaz, Golding and Cascade as if they were Chardonnay, Cabernet and Malbec. Brewers even speak of the four 'noble' hop varieties, just as winemakers speak in hushed tones of certain 'noble' grapes. You, of course, can name these as the classic lager hops, Hallertauer Mittelfrüh, Tettnanger and Spalter from Germany and Saaz from the Czech Republic. Add that these noble hops are prized more for their aroma (delicate, floral and spicy) than for their, albeit gentle, bitterness.

Indeed, some brewers are experimenting with single-hop-variety beers, following the example of single-grape-variety New World wines, but you must argue that these are seldom as balanced and harmonious as beers made with a well-judged blend of hop varieties.

When discussing the role of hops in beer, add gravitas to your comments by occasionally referring to them by their scientific name, Humulus lupulus, which, you must explain, means 'wolf plant'. Hops are so named because, left unchecked, they spread voraciously, devouring (okay, choking) any other plants that get in their way.

While barley provides the body to beer, hops provide the much-needed seasoning. Without the bitter, dry and aromatic contribution from hops, most beers would be overly sweet, malty and one-dimensional, lacking in balance and complexity. Typically, a barrel of beer is made from about 20kg (44lb) of malt to a mere 150g (5.5oz) of hops. Describe it as a symbiotic relationship akin to cake (malt) and icing (hops).

And, of course, any fool knows that it's only the larger female hop flowers that are used in brewing. These flowers, called 'cones', contain alpha and beta acids, which provide bitterness, and hop oils, which give resinous, citric and floral aromas.

Just as malted barley has earned its place as the brewer's grain of choice, so hops have become the go-to seasoning. Other herbs, fruits and spices that have been added to beer to give it that *je ne sais quoi* over the centuries include rosemary, ginger, liquorice, thistles, ivy, sage, nutmeg, aniseed and good old bog myrtle. Various combinations were often blended together to make the seasoning mixture called 'gruit'. And let's not forget that Belgian brewers are famed for their superb fruit beers and wheat beers, the latter spiced with coriander, cumin and dried orange peel. Observe knowledgeably that history is going full circle with trendy craft brewers now experimenting with the likes of poppy seeds, chestnuts, chilli peppers and juniper. Hops, however, have one very significant advantage over these other additives. They don't just balance out the sweetness of malt, they also have antibacterial, preservative qualities that prevent beer from spoiling.

'He was a wise man who invented beer.'

Plato

Closely related to both the humble nettle and cannabis, hops were used in the olden days to treat migraines, bedwetting and leprosy – with mixed results. Stuffed into pillows, hops have also been used to ward off insomnia, and they are still used in herbal sleep remedies today. Hops have even been attributed with aphrodisiac qualities, again providing much-needed balance, only in this instance against the 'brewer's-droop' effect caused by over-imbibing.

Specific types of hops are used for specific effects at various stages in the brewing process. 'Bittering hops' with high alpha acid content are generally introduced at an early stage, when the wort is boiling in the brew kettle. 'Finishing hops', rich in aromatic hop oils, are added late in the boil ('late hopping') to give a range of spicy and citric qualities. And traditional British ales are often 'dry hopped', which involves throwing some 'finishing hops' into the maturation cask, boosting the heady, hoppy perfume to the max.

Hops come in a wide range of handy formats, from whole dried hop flowers and pressure-formed pellets (which make it much easier to clean out the copper) to fresh hops, rushed straight from the hop bine before they (quickly) deteriorate. Beers made with fresh hops are called 'wet-hop' or 'green-hop' beers. The use of hop extracts in liquid form is cheating, rather like adding wood chips to wine. In the brewery, sacks of hops are called 'pockets'. You are now frighteningly well versed in hop terminology, so it's time to brush up on your hop varieties on a need-to-know basis.

As well as the four noble hop varieties previously mentioned, you need to be familiar with the English hops, Fuggle and Golding. These are the Morecambe and Wise of the hop world: hugely popular, with Fuggle (an earthy, grassy, bittering hop) playing the straight man, and Golding (aromatic, zesty and floral) bringing the sunshine. Golding is largely responsible for the rich marmalade notes of traditional English ales. Kent and Hereford, of course, are the hop gardens of England.

Most American hops are cultivated in the Yakima Valley in Washington and the Willamette Valley in Oregon. Refer to them as 'the three 'Cs' – Cascade, Chinook and Columbus. And be aware that you cannot mention American hops without commenting on their particularly aggressive resinous and citrus traits, best summed up as in-your-face grapefruit, which is their trademark. Synonymous with the American craft brewing movement, they're used by the bucket-load in staggeringly bitter yet fragrant pale ales and IPAs. Express concern, however, that some new-wave American brewers seem locked in a bitter(!) battle to out-hop each other, as shown by the astonishingly high IBU of their brews. IBU, of course, stands for International Bittering Units, which is a measurement, funnily enough, of 'units of bitterness'. Brutally hopped 'Double' IPAs, for example, might have 65 or more IBU, while cheap 'lawnmower'* lager could have a measly 10 IBU. An IBU rating is arrived at via a complex calculation based on the weight of hops, alpha acids, wort and alcohol. Deliver your bluffing *coup de grâce* by patiently explaining that one IBU is equivalent to one milligram of alpha acid per litre of beer. Then remind your listener that it's their round.

YEASTIE BOYS

As you now know, barley gives body to a beer and hops the seasoning, but yeast is the final arbiter of style. Ultimately, the strain of yeast selected by the brewer will do more to influence the overall style and flavour of his brew than any of the other ingredients. It's ironic, therefore, that yeast was the last piece of the brewing jigsaw to be identified and understood. Because yeast is invisible to the naked eye, the process of fermentation was regarded

---

* 'Lawnmower' beer is a derogatory term used by aficionados to describe beers so bland that they are good only for chugging, perhaps while mowing the lawn.

as something miraculous, a divine gift called 'God is good'. It wasn't until 1857 that Louis Pasteur blew yeast's cover, identifying it, not as a magic ingredient, but as a single-cell microorganism, a tiny fungus, that consumes sugars to create alcohol and carbon dioxide. And in 1883, Emil Christian Hansen, working at the Carlsberg brewery in Copenhagen, managed to isolate and cultivate a single pure strain of yeast, which he called Saccharomyces carlsbergensis.

Before these discoveries, brewers would source their yeast by skimming it off the latest batch of beer, which of course left the yeast open to mutation and infection. Nowadays, brewers employ microbiologists, who quite possibly wear oversized glasses like Brains in *Thunderbirds,* to store their unique and irreplaceable yeast strains in 'yeast banks'. Some devil-may-care brewers, notably in Belgium, still prefer to use wild yeasts of the Brettanomyces genus. They leave their fermentation tanks open to the elements to invite these airborne beasties in. These feral yeasts have their wild way with the wort, creating the distinctively sour, farmyardy flavours found in lambic beers and the traditional red and brown ales of Flanders.

While there might be dozens of grain combinations and a few hundred hops to choose from, there are thousands of yeast strains. There are, however, two basic forms of brewer's yeast: ale yeast (Saccharomyces cerevisiae) and lager yeast (Saccharomyces pastorianus, named after Pasteur). Saccharomyces, rather cutely, means 'sugar fungus'.

As you can explain to your rapt saloon-bar audience,

ale yeast and lager yeast behave quite differently during fermentation. Ale yeasts rise to the top of the tank, gorging on sugars in a frenzy of foam, heat and fury, reminiscent of piranhas at work, which generally lasts about two to four days. Lager yeasts, on the other hand, work best in very cool conditions, sinking to the bottom of the tank where they slowly nibble away at the sugars for up to two weeks. This is why ales are described as 'top-fermented', and lagers as 'bottom-fermented'. It's easy to remember, as bottom-fermented lager tends to be gassier, with odious consequences in the trouser department. Those of a more genteel persuasion prefer to focus on the temperatures at which these yeasts operate, and so refer to the beers as 'warm-fermented' (ale) and 'cold-fermented' (lager). Ale yeasts are much more picky eaters, leaving more of the sugars behind, which is why ales tend to be sweeter, fuller-bodied and fruitier than lagers.

For ease of reference, the principal top-fermented styles include ales, stouts, porters, wheat beers and lambics. Bottom-fermented, sorry, cold-fermented beers include the full spectrum of lager styles, from bocks to Pilsners.

WATER PALAVER

Water is the wet stuff in beer, accounting for some 95% of even the strongest, most headbanging brews. But even with something as seemingly simple as water, there is ample scope for bluffing because – hooray! – even water is no simple matter when it comes to brewing.

The mineral content of water has an enormous influence

on the style of beer. Particularly useful brewing minerals include sodium chloride (salt) which intensifies flavour; calcium sulphate which encourages extraction from malt and hops, aiding fermentation; magnesium sulphate which stimulates yeast; and calcium chloride which enhances sweetness and body.

A beer's style is greatly influenced by the local water, explaining why historical centres of brewing like London and Burton upon Trent, Pilsen in the Czech Republic, and Dublin sprang up where they did. The particularly hard waters of London and Burton, with plenty of mineral salts and sulphates, are ideal for making pale ales and IPAs. If you're feeling brave, you can refer to the distinct dryness and vaguely sulphuric aroma of Burton's ales, caused by high levels of calcium sulphate in the water, as 'Burton snatch'. High levels of chloride enhance the sweetness of Dublin's dark stouts, and Pilsner's soft drinkability reflects the soft water (low in carbonates, bicarbonate and sulphates) of its Bohemian birthplace.

Thanks to technological advances like reverse osmosis, brewers nowadays can manipulate water's mineral content to the extent that they can make pretty much any style of beer anywhere they like. This enables them to recreate non-local beer styles wherever they hang their hat, which has, of course, played a significant role in the international spread of the craft brewing movement. Recreating the gypsum and magnesium-rich waters of Burton upon Trent, for example, for pale ale and IPA production, is known as 'Burtonisation'.

From stimulating germination in the grain to sluicing out fermentation tanks, it's estimated that five pints of water are needed to make just one pint of beer. But do remember that water used in the actual brewing process is always referred to as 'liquor'. 'Water' is the stuff they hose down the floors with.

BLOWING THE FROTH OFF: SERVING BEER

Few drinking experiences plumb the depths of disappointment like flat, warm beer. Yes, even in England – and especially in the summertime. Would the ending of *Ice Cold in Alex* have been quite so poignant if Johnny Mills's beer had been tepid and lifeless? Beer's greatest enemies are heat, light and oily residues, all of which can kill the moment, but few issues are as emotive as 'the head'.

HEAD FIRST

The foam on your beer is produced by proteins in malted barley, and contains a concentration of hop oils bound up in the bubbles. These oils help to stabilise the head and enable it to cling to the sides of the glass, producing the coveted 'lacing' effect as the beer goes down. As discussed in the tasting section, a sip from the head provides a revealing snapshot of the hop oils and bitterness in your beer.

You will notice that the head on a cask-conditioned beer comprises very large bubbles (carbon dioxide foam), while the head on a nitrokeg beer has tiny, much finer bubbles (nitrogen foam). This enables you to perform the impressive feat of telling a cask-conditioned beer from a nitrokeg beer by appearance alone.

Some argue that a resplendent head keeps the beer beneath both fresh and fizzy, which makes you wonder how long it takes them to finish a pint. Others suggest that a foaming head performs no function at all – that it is merely a question of aesthetics. The jury's still out on this one, but you can argue that it's a textural thing; it's just so much nicer drinking beer through bubbles.

Assuming you do value your head, here's how to keep yours while others around you might be losing theirs. Any form of oily residue will break up the foam on your beer, so glasses should be squeaky clean with no traces of foambusting detergent. Avoid peanuts, crisps and other fatty snacks, as even traces of oil on your lips can dissipate the head. Should a rogue peanut fall into your pint, you can kiss your head goodbye, and trying to fish it out with your (oily) fingers will only make matters worse. And go easy on the lipstick.

With regards to size, the head shouldn't be much more than half an inch thick, so take it back if you feel shortchanged. While the continentals serve up some beers with heads so thick and foaming that a chocolate flake wouldn't look out of place, most of the head is usually above the rim of the glass, so it shouldn't be a cause for complaint.

The next time you're observing the world through the bottom of a pint glass, look out for criss-cross patterns or branded messages on the inner base. These markings are pitted with tiny holes (nucleated) to increase the formation of bubbles, thus retaining the head. Without these small pits, it is estimated that a regular pint glass would keep its head for no more than three or four minutes.

Should a rogue peanut fall into your pint, you can kiss your head goodbye.

Which leads us to the wonderful world of widgets. Resembling a very small ping-pong ball with a tiny hole in it, a widget creates a smooth nitrogen foam when a can of beer is opened, imitating the head on draught beer. The can is filled under pressure with nitrogen so that some of the gas fills the widget through the hole. When the can is opened the pressure is released and the gas escapes through the hole, creating a stream of bubbles in the beer. The original widget was patented by Guinness in 1969.

POUR SHOW

If you're drinking bottled beer, the desired half-inch head hinges on how you pour it. For best results, pour beer as you would champagne, lemonade or any other carbonated drink. Hold the glass at an angle of 45 degrees and pour your beer, slowly and steadily, onto a spot roughly halfway up the side of the glass. As the beer hits this sweet spot, slowly tilt your glass into the upright position. So far, so simple.

The more interesting question when pouring bottle-conditioned beers is whether you want to drink the yeast sediment or not. Of course, a bit of yeast never hurt anyone; it actually contains vitamins that are good for your skin, hair, nails and liver. Having said this, some yeast sediments are scrummier than others. The yeasts in some Belgian beers are so pleasantly fruity that they are poured with gay abandon into the glass. In fact, there's a saying in Belgium that the top two-thirds of the bottle are for the head and heart, and the bottom third, with all the yeasty bits, is for the stomach.

If you don't want any sediment in your beer, gently roll the beer bottle on the bar-top before pouring. Explain to any interested observers that this pre-pouring ritual helps to bind the yeast sediment together, making it easier to leave it behind in the bottle.

Should you want lots of yeast sediment in your glass, you will need to perform the classic wheat-beer pour, also known as The Hefeweizen Maneuver (*hefeweizen* being German for cloudy wheat beer). Most wheat beers, as you know, are meant to be drunk cloudy, with their yeast swirling about in the glass. Start pouring as you would any other beer but when about three-quarters of the beer has been poured – and you are sure that you have an appreciative audience – stop pouring, wipe your brow, and gently swirl the bottle to 'catch' any stubborn yeast clinging to the bottom of the bottle. Do not over-swirl as you will end up with a bottle of foam. Your beer will become noticeably cloudier, and yeastier, when you pour in this final quarter. If nobody has noticed your performance, lift your glass to the light to admire your handiwork.

GLASSWARE

Nobody understands the importance of glass design and function quite like the Belgians, who seem to have a bespoke glass for each and every beer. Many Belgian beer glasses are tulip-, chalice- or goblet-shaped, like chunky, oversized wine glasses. When held by the stem, the beer within stays cooler for longer, unwarmed by hands, and bigger versions are ideal for retaining a large, creamy head. But perhaps most importantly, a wine-glass shape is best suited for the appreciation of aroma, allowing for much theatrical swirling between inhalations and exclamations. Form and function combine.

Similarly, the tall, tapered shape of traditional Pilsner glasses borrows heavily from the champagne flute, allowing us to admire the fine streams of bubbles as they rise up the glass. Tall, vase-like wheat-beer glasses allow a thick head to form, while aiding the even distribution of suspended yeast particles for the full cloudy effect.

Traditional British pint glasses are admirably suited for the dual functions of 'getting lots in' and 'necking it', without any pause for thought or admiring the bouquet. Refer to a straight-sided British pint glass as a 'sleeve', or 'sleever' in the West Country; and remark on how the traditional dimpled design of a handled pint glass shows the glinting bronze and copper hues of British bitter to best effect. The handle, of course, also keeps warm hands away from the glass.

'Beauty is in the eye of the beer holder.'

Kinky Friedman

Ordering a Kwak, a dark, strong Belgian beer, will inspire glass-envy in any crowded bar. It's traditionally served in a round-bottomed flask, like something from a laboratory, standing in its own wooden holder. Explain that this unique receptacle dates back to Napoleonic times, when mail-coach drivers were forbidden from stopping for a beer. Cunning brewer, Pauwel Kwak, solved the problem by designing a glass that could be hung from a wooden holder attached to the side of a coach, which lends a whole new meaning to 'nipping out for a swifty'.

SERVING TEMPERATURES

It is a myth perpetrated by Australians that the Brits drink warm beer. This is pretty rich coming from a culture where beer is considered too warm unless your lips are frozen to the 'tinny'; and aimed at the country responsible for about a third of the classic beer styles. Pity such ignorance and patiently explain that while lagers, like white wines, benefit from cooler temperatures, fuller-bodied ales, like fine red wines, are best enjoyed at 'cellar temperature', which is somewhere between 10 and 14 degrees centigrade – which is not warm. Point out that chilling beer enhances refreshment and carbonation, at the expense of flavour, while warmer temperatures enhance sweetness, aroma and body.

Beers that blossom at cellar temperature include cask-conditioned ales, porters and stouts, mild, Trappist ales, and lambics. You can go slightly warmer (cool room temperature, about 16 degrees centigrade) with vintage beers, old ale, barley wine and Imperial stout. Wheat beers, golden and blonde ales, pale ales, IPAs and most British bitters can handle a light chill (8 to 12 degrees). At the other end of the scale, most lagers should be served well chilled (4 to 8 degrees). Beers that are chilled to within an inch of their lives (below 4 degrees) taste of precisely nothing, making it the ideal serving temperature for many Australian lagers.

STORAGE

Probably the closest you'll get to cellar temperature, in the absence of an actual cellar, is your garage; which you must, naturally, refer to as your cellar. It's where you keep your extensive collection of bottle-conditioned, old and vintage ales, barley wines, Imperial stouts and porters, and Belgian Trappist ales. Of course, most beer is designed to be drunk within a few hours of getting it through the door, but these robust, high-alcohol styles, some with yeast sediment, will mature gracefully, developing greater complexity over a year or two.

Keep a watchful eye on the sell-by date of 'hop-forward' beers (those with lots of hops), because hop oils are quite volatile and sensitive. Their delicate floral and resiny aromas are susceptible to oxygen and will fade dramatically if left for too long.

Most bottles should be stored upright, as beer will degrade crown-cap seals over time. And you certainly don't want to keep bottle-conditioned beers laying down, as the yeast sediment will collect halfway up the bottle, making them tricky to pour. Corked bottles, on the other hand, should be stored horizontally to prevent their corks from drying out, leading to oxidation. They should be restored to the perpendicular a couple of days before drinking to allow any yeast sediment to settle.

In the absence of a cellar or garage, you should store bottled beers in as dry, dark and cool a place as you can find – perhaps a cupboard under the stairs. It's important that this space remains at a consistent temperature, so beware radiators and heating pipes. Consistently cool is better than cold with warm spells.

BOTTLES OR CANS?

Where does the bluffer stand on the thorny issue of bottles versus cans? It's true that cans have developed something of a pile 'em high, sell 'em cheap reputation, but these days even trendy craft brewers are beginning to see the benefits of 'tinnies'. Some people swear blind that bottled beer tastes better and, specifically, less metallic than canned beer. Suggest that this might be a psychological hurdle, seeing as the vast majority of beer cans are lined with an inert plasticky lacquer to prevent any contact with metal. Bottles and cans are both recyclable, but cans are cheaper and lighter. Bottles have more aesthetic appeal, which is an important part of beer appreciation.

Choose your weapons.

'I liked the taste of the beer, its live white lather, its brass-bright depths, the sudden world through the wet brown walls of the glass, the tilted rush to the lips and the slow swallowing down to the lapping belly, the salt on the tongue, the foam at the corners.'

Dylan Thomas

A QUESTION OF TASTE

In the traditional beer-drinking cultures of northern and central Europe and North America, beer rather suffers in comparison with wine's ooh-la-la image. Of course, the boot's on the other foot in the traditional wine belt, where a chilled bottle of imported lager, perhaps with gothic script, seems impossibly exotic beside a plastic flagon of fermented grape juice. But in beer's homelands, ale is seen as an honest drink to be drunk after an honest day's work, a blue-collar beverage not afraid to roll up its sleeves and get stuck in. We quaff it when we have a genuine thirst to quench, not when we're seeking the perfect match for goat's cheese roulade with a raspberry coulis.

Unreconstructed lager louts still view wine nerds with deep suspicion, looking on disdainfully as they splash around in their ocean of adjectives. But you, beer bluffer par excellence, sitting atop your ivory pump handle, know better. With your 'hard-earned' knowledge of beer's rich diversity, you know it's high time that beer drinkers jumped in too, and that the water's lovely once you're in. Of course, there's a world of difference between quaffing a few ales with your mates down the pub (drinking) and full-blown organoleptic analysis (tasting). Most of us can cope with the former, but struggle with the latter, so here are some tips:

- The golden rule of beer tasting – and you're probably going to like this – is always swallow. Do not, on any account, spit it out like wine tasters. This obviously limits the number of beers you can – ahem – 'taste' with a clear head, but your excuse is cast iron. Hop character, bitterness and dryness are accentuated by swallowing, due to the positioning of bitterness receptors at the back of the throat and tongue. ('It was the bitterness receptors that made me do it, Your Honour.')

- Never try to taste beer from a can, a bottle or a full pint glass. You won't be able to appreciate the subtle hue of your brew in a can or bottle, and if you swirl a pint glass to release your beer's aromas (an essential part of the tasting process), you're likely to drench everyone within a five-foot radius, winning you no friends and making the pub floor stickier than it already is.

- No, the best vessel for swirling and tasting beer – oh, the irony – is a decent-sized wine glass, or a chalice/goblet-shaped beer glass, as favoured by the civilised Belgians. And speaking of civilised, any decent real-ale pub should happily give you a small taster of any beer that whets your curiosity. There are, of course, sensible limits; don't push your luck looking for second opinions.

SEE, SNIFF, SWALLOW

Having established tasting etiquette and the right tools for the job, let's get to work:

- The first assessment of beer should be visual because, it's true, we do eat and drink 'with our eyes'. And a beer's colour should give you a good indication of its style. At the very least, it should appear clear and bright, unless it's a wheat beer, in which case cloudy is cool. Is your Pilsner sufficiently golden and sparkling, your stout sufficiently dark and opaque? Does your barley wine or bitter light up the room with its amber, come-hither glow? Does the head retain its structure, leaving a delicate 'lace' down the side of your glass? You get the picture. Hold your glass against a white wall or up to the light for best results – and maximum dramatic effect.

- Next up, perform the aforementioned swirl to aerate your beer, awakening the aromas from their slumber. Take a deep, self-satisfied sniff, making sure you are being observed. Here, you can pontificate on the relative merits of nose and tongue as instruments of analysis. Berate the tongue as a dim-witted charlatan, capable of detecting only four basic sensations – sweetness, bitterness, sourness and saltiness. Extol the virtues of your nasal cavities, especially the olfactory bulb perched at the top, which is capable of detecting thousands of tiny nuances. This is why a blocked nose robs us of our sense of taste. Can you smell the calling-card clove and bubblegum of wheat beer? Are you getting the tangy, bittersweet marmalade aromas of a cheeky ale? The espresso coffee and bitter chocolate of burly stout and porter? Or the floral delicacy of a Pilsner, skittish as a startled fawn? If, as Robert Louis Stevenson once remarked, 'Wine is bottled poetry', then beer is bottled prose, and it's long overdue a purple patch.

- You're probably getting pretty thirsty by now and your friends have likely moved on to the next pub, so it's time you actually put some beer in your mouth. Not too much, as you want to be able to suck in some air, as if whistling backwards, without actually choking. Don't forget to swallow. Obviously, you'll pick up on some basic flavours, but here you're assessing bitterness, texture ('mouthfeel') and finish. To really impress your friends (if any of them are still left), ask the barman for a spoon so you can sample a little of the froth on top your beer. Hop oils concentrate here, allowing you to gauge hop flavours and bitterness quite separately from the rest of the beer.

- In terms of texture and finish, is your beer creamy or thin, full-, medium- or light-bodied, sparkling, gassy or flat? Is it warming or refreshing? Does it glide over your tongue like a silk scarf, or is it a tad 'chewy'? When it comes to the finish, does your beer reveal its character in tantalising layers, like a dance of the seven veils? Do the flavours vanish as quickly as a

Premier League footballer from a poetry reading? Or do they linger on, stretching towards a hoppy, hazy horizon with soft, fluffy clouds of malt?

LET'S TALK FLAVOUR

This brings us to 'malty' and 'hoppy', unquestionably the most overused yet utterly useless descriptors for the flavours of beer. Right up there with 'grapey' for wine or 'beefy', as used in connection with beef, their use on beer labels is shamefully lazy; about as helpful as 'traditionally brewed' or 'the true taste of Olde England'. Apologists argue that the language of beer is in its infancy, and it's true that back labels are becoming much more informative, but 'malty' and 'hoppy' show all the linguistic development of 'goo-goo' and 'ga-ga'. Yes, wine labels can be absurdly flowery, but why should beer drinkers be confronted by labels as enlightening as the Enigma code?

It is a cop-out to describe beers simply as 'malty' and 'hoppy'.

All of this gives the aspiring beer bluffer the opportunity to shine. Malt and hops are, indeed, the dominant factors in beer's flavour profile, but there are so many shades of malt and different hop varieties that it is a cop-out to describe beers simply as 'malty' and 'hoppy'. Even the most diehard real-ale fanatics will admit that it requires practice, but try to be more specific about the malt and hop characteristics you encounter. What kind of malt characteristics does your beer have? Does it remind you of caramel, honey, treacle, molasses, chocolate, coffee, smoke, liquorice or raisins? If hops are the defining characteristic of your beer, describe it as 'hop forward', then cast around for specific hop aromas. Is it floral, grassy or earthy? Can you smell geranium, nettles, pine resin or citrus fruit? And if citrus fruit is to the fore, is it orange, lemon or grapefruit?

If you need a steer, many British pubs have adopted the Cyclops system for describing their real ales. Launched in 2006 by the Campaign for Real Ale (CAMRA) and a host of participating breweries, it's called Cyclops after its logo depicting a nose (for smell), mouth (taste) and a single eye (sight). You might have seen it on various pump handles. Each beer submitted to the Cyclops tasting panel is awarded points out of five for sweetness and bitterness (think malt and hops), and is then described with no more than three words each for 'appearance', 'smell' and 'taste'. Thus, Sunchaser Blonde from Everards has a sweetness rating of three, and bitterness of one and a half. Appearance is 'gold straw'; smell is 'delicate, citrus fruit'; and taste is 'subtle, zesty, sweet'. Check out the website (www.cyclopsbeer.co.uk) for its database of real-ale tasting notes. It's a useful tool with simple vocabulary.

Your motives for wanting to describe your beer might arise from a genuine desire to record your favourite brands and styles for future reference, or from a more primeval urge to show off. We're not here to judge you.

WHEELY INTERESTING

Back in the 1970s, a bunch of beardy beer boffins convened at the Brewing Industry Research Foundation in Surrey, England, to reinvent the wheel. They devised the 'Beer Flavour Wheel', a massive pie chart with each segment describing the aromas, flavours and textures commonly found in beer. Their aim was to create a standard international currency of beer adjectives. Whether they succeeded or not is a moot point, but here are some of the more useful segments with corresponding adjectives –

Aromatic	spicy, vinous
Estery	banana, apple, bubblegum
Fruity	lemon, apple, pear
Floral	rose, perfume
Resinous/grassy	fresh-cut grass, hay
Nutty	walnut, coconut, almond
Grainy	malt, straw
Roasted	caramel, liquorice, burnt, smoked, bread crust
Phenolic	tarry
Soapy, oily	cheesy, sweaty, buttery
Sulphury	struck match, rotten eggs, burnt rubber, cooked vegetables
Oxidised	stale, musty, catty, sherry-like, cardboardy, earthy
Sour	vinegar, sour milk
Sweet	honey, vanilla, jam

ORIGINAL GRAVITY

Indulging in a spot of beer banter provides the ideal opportunity to display your knowledge of 'original gravity'. It might sound like a prog rock album title, but original gravity is actually a measurement used by brewers to calculate a beer's eventual strength. Yes, we know that ABV (alcohol by volume), as printed on a label, does a pretty good job of telling you how strong a beer actually is, but where's the fun in something that's easily comprehensible? Define OG as a reading of the weight of the wort before fermentation against the weight of the water, thus indicating the amount of fermentable sugars in the brew before the yeast sets to work. Thus, bearing in mind that water has a gravity of 1.000, beer with an original gravity of 1.040 will probably end up at about 4% alcohol (ABV).

If this leaves your beer buddies reeling, hit them with the following: the Continental equivalents to original gravity are degrees Plato and degrees Balling. As they plead for mercy, finish them off with a swift uppercut: to convert a degrees Plato or Balling figure to an approximate OG, just multiply by four. Thus, a 10-degree Balling/Plato beer would have an OG of 1.040. Simple.

WHEN GOOD BEERS TURN BAD: SPOTTING FAULTS

Sadly, there might come a time when your anticipated reverie of honey and freshly cut grass is rudely interrupted by an 'off' smell like rotten vegetables or vinegar. Rather than concealing your disappointment, you must have the confidence to identify faults in your beer and ask for a replacement.

One of the most common 'off' smells is wet cardboard, which is an indication that your beer is oxidised. Either it's past its sell-by date or it hasn't been stored properly, allowing excessive contact with oxygen, which makes it taste stale. A sherry-like, malt vinegar whiff can also indicate oxidation, unless of course you're drinking a lambic beer, in which case it is to be admired. Describe this smell as acetic.

Cask-conditioned ales shouldn't hang around for more than a month, and you wouldn't want to drink in a pub where this would be allowed to happen anyway.

Broadly speaking, cask-conditioned ales shouldn't really hang around for more than a month, and you wouldn't want to drink in a pub where this would be allowed to happen anyway. If cask-conditioned ale is flat, insipid and generally lacking in character, it's an indication that the cask has passed its drink-by date. Some beers, like vintage ales and dark seasonal brews, suit maturity. Their higher alcohol levels make them more robust and fuller-bodied, so that they 'fade' more slowly. As a rule of thumb, keg beers will last for at least six weeks, while bottles and cans can be left for up to a year, not that this is likely to happen.

Unusual vegetal smells like celery or parsnip could be a sign of bacterial infection, while unpleasant whiffs of plastic, TCP or creosote indicate wild yeast infection.

Excessive foaming, known as 'gushing', is another indication of infection or old age. It could also mean the beer has been served too warm, but either way it's undrinkable, and you should say so. Vesuvius is a bad look for any beer.

A hint of toffee or caramel can be a good thing, but an excessively sweet butterscotch smell in lager would imply to the seasoned drinker that either fermentation or maturation/conditioning has been cut short. Affected lagers are disappointingly lacking in the refreshment department. Describe overly sweet butterscotch smells as 'diacetyl' (a good brewing word, pronounced di-as-eh-til).

If bottled beers are exposed to too much light, their hop oils degrade, a condition known as 'lightstrike' or 'sunstrike', which produces peculiar vegetal, rubbery or wet dog smells. Some refer to this whiff as 'skunky', but having never been up close and personal with a skunk, this writer couldn't possibly comment. Observe that brown glass is the most effective in countering lightstrike, followed by green glass. Clear glass, obviously, is completely useless.

Perhaps the most misunderstood 'fault' in beer is cloudiness, which can mean all sorts of things. Most wheat beers, of course, are meant to be cloudy. It could indicate, however, that a cask-conditioned beer hasn't been given sufficient time to 'drop'. In other words, the yeast that has been introduced to spark a secondary fermentation has not had the chance to settle. It could also mean you're drinking the end of the barrel. Unless you have access to the cellar, you're unlikely to know. Cask-conditioned beer can also develop a faint cloudiness called 'hop haze' or 'chill haze' if served too cold. In all these instances, provided the beer tastes fresh, it won't harm you. Nasty flavours, on the other hand, would indicate bacteria in suspension and should be avoided. Let your nose be your guide.

'You can't be a real country unless you have a beer and an airline. It helps if you have some kind of a football team, or some nuclear weapons, but at the very least you need a beer.'

Frank Zappa

BEERS AROUND THE WORLD

At this point you can bluff your way through the history of beer, how it works, and what to do with it, but now it's time for the nitty-gritty. Your saloon-bar status will stand or fall according to your knowledge of the classic beer styles. Thanks to the craft-beer revolution (read on), pretty much every style is made pretty much everywhere, wherever men and women dare to dream – and to drink. Here, however, each style is presented according to the country where it originated. In very broad terms, the Brits perfected ale, the Germans blessed us with lager, which the Czechs turned into liquid gold, while those crazy Belgians are to beer what the French are to wine. The following chapters detail the nations which are central to the history and development of beer, and as a bluffer you need to know why.

Europe is the cradle of all of the popular beer styles, which were spread through colonial expansion in the eighteenth century and mass emigration to America in the nineteenth century. Beer is now universal, the world's favourite drink (bluffers should never use the word 'beverage'), but one style has travelled much better than the rest. We are talking, of course, about lager, which even the most embittered ale anorak would have to admit offers refreshment beyond the call of duty. Indeed, in hotter climates, this is sometimes beer's only duty.

Lager arrived in America with a wave of German immigrants in the late nineteenth century. While the German predilection for leather shorts and oompah bands remained a niche prospect, lager spread across the new continent as quickly as the railroads. Among these German settlers were men like Eberhard Anheuser, Adolphus Busch, Frederick Pabst, Frederick Miller, Joseph Schlitz and Adolph Coors, all of whom became household names.

They developed lagers using local ingredients, including corn and rice, which don't offer the same body and flavour as barley, but which accelerated the brewing process to satisfy a seemingly unquenchable thirst. Maturation and conditioning times were shortened, and it became standard practice to filter and pasteurise. Flavour took a back seat as brand loyalties, buoyed by massive advertising campaigns, took root. By 1910, the USA was the world's largest beer producer, though it has since slipped to second place behind China. Russia is currently third, followed by Brazil – always worth dropping into any beer-related conversation.

Lager reached Australia when the Foster brothers – from America, incidentally – opened their brewery in Melbourne in 1888. They brought big-time American brewing techniques with them and used local ingredients, including sugar cane, which helps to explain why Aussie lagers tend to be on the sweeter side. China, Japan, India, Thailand and Indonesia all have their own lager brands, which are generally rice-based, light and refreshing.

In the ale heartlands of Britain, the snappily named Austro-Bavarian Lager Beer Brewery and Crystal Ice Factory established a beachhead for lager in London in 1881, and in 1885 the Tennent's brewery set the ball rolling in Scotland. By the 1960s, heavily advertised lager had made serious inroads into both the British Isles and British ales, prompting the formation of CAMRA (Campaign for Real Ale) in 1971. While lager nowadays accounts for some 80% of beers drunk worldwide, it's closer to 60% in Britain, where traditional ales and porters are now standing their ground.

After English and Cantonese, lager is probably the third international language, yet for the worst beer snobs it remains the 'L' word. Don't make this mistake. You can drink original Pilsners, golden helles, dark dunkels and rich, malty bocks, for example, with your head held high. For beer connoisseurs (read 'bluffers'), lager is not the enemy; bland, mass-produced commodity beers are.

'Beer is the reason I get up in the afternoon.'

Anon

BREWING FOR BRITAIN

PALE ALE AND INDIA PALE ALE

After lager, pale ale must be the most loosely defined of all beer styles, being the generic term for ales that happen to be pale. To be a little more precise, it applies to a family of hoppy, copper-coloured, bitter beers that includes English and American pale ales, India Pale Ales (IPAs), Double and Imperial IPAs, a smattering of Belgian ales and English bitter. English beers, it seems, are defined by their degrees of brownness, and, relatively speaking, pale ale is less brown than – well – brown ale.

The 'pale' bit specifically refers to the colour of the malt used to make this broad style. Going back to the metaphorical Dark (brown) Ages, most English beers were a deep shade of brown, made from brown and amber malts, but this changed big time with the arrival of coke-fired kilns in the mid-eighteenth century. These offered much greater control than traditional coal-fired kilns, enabling maltsters to fine-tune their roasting techniques to produce lightly roasted pale malts. This is the sort of historical insight that all beer bluffers should have at their fingertips. With brewing centred in London and Burton upon Trent, where the hard, mineral-rich waters accentuate hop bitterness, pale ales were suddenly all the rage.

It became apparent, however, that pale ales were simply too pale to withstand the gruelling voyage to the colonies in India. Circa 1790, George Hodgson of London created a much more robust, turbo-charged version that came to be known as India Pale Ale (IPA). At around 7% ABV, traditional IPA was much stronger than run-of-the-mill pale ale, and was packed to the gunwales with hops for their antibacterial, preservative qualities. If in doubt, describe IPA as a 'hop-forward' style.

During the First and Second World Wars, due to restrictions on raw materials and the need for clear-headed munitions workers, the strength of many British beers was greatly reduced. While the thriving microbrewing movement is helping to restore some lost pride, many British beers are still pale imitations of the original versions, and IPA is no exception. The only true survivor of the original IPA style is the spicy, marmaladey Worthington White Shield (5.6%) from Burton upon Trent. You can point out, however, that Meantime IPA from Greenwich in London and Burton Bridge Empire Pale Ale, both bitingly bitter and weighing in at 7.4% and 7.5%, respectively, are also worthy standard-bearers. As an IPA aficionado, you must complain that anything much weaker is simply letting the side down.

For this very reason you are a big fan of the macho pale ale and IPA variants now arriving from the USA. For the last 30 years or so, the American craft beer movement has been brewing up the thinking man's alternative to bland beer, the antidote to anodyne ales. New-wave American brewers have drawn inspiration from classic European beer styles, and have created their own high-octane interpretations. In the movement's early years, many adopted English pale ales and IPAs for their 'brew-prints', and they are now giving them back with interest. The Sierra Nevada Brewing Company of Chico, California, is widely regarded as the US pale ale pioneer, having launched its now iconic, assertively spicy Sierra Nevada Pale Ale (5.6%) in 1980.

As you now know, American hop varieties such as Cascade, Chinook and Columbus are renowned for their intensely aromatic, resinous and citrus (especially grapefruit) qualities. In fact, if you ever detect strong hints of grapefruit in a beer, it's usually worth a punt to suggest that it might come from American hops. It's easy to see why these pungent beauties and British IPA were a special relationship waiting to happen and, together, they're making beers that are resin-ating around the world.

Now, of course, some English brewers are returning the compliment by lacing their own beers with American hops. Meantime London Pale Ale (4.3%), for example, combines lashings of American Cascade and Centennial hops with good old Kentish Goldings.

While you maintain a fashionable enthusiasm for the American craft brewing scene, you should express some concern over hopping that might be a little heavy-handed.

Suggest that the American belief that 'bigger is better, but bitter is best' is in danger of escalating out of control as brewers compete to out-hop each other. True to form, the Americans have created two new IPA styles called Double and Imperial IPA, which can be alarmingly bitter.

PORTER AND STOUT

The origins of porter are as dark and opaque as the beer itself. Still, there's no harm in you regaling your drinking buddies with the tale of Ralph Harwood while they're waiting for their pints to settle. It was common practice in the early eighteenth century for London's landlords to serve customers with a blend of beers from different butts, mixed on the premises. Each beer was referred to as a 'thread', with 'three threads' (a blend of three beers) proving most popular. This allowed landlords to blend threads according to the punter's choice, and to offload dodgy brews without anyone noticing. The story goes that Mr Harwood, owner of the Bell Brewhouse in Shoreditch, East London, 'invented' what came to be known as porter in 1722 by helping out the landlord of the nearby Blue Last pub on Great Eastern Street. Allegedly, Harwood came up with a dark, labour-saving beer in the style of the landlord's most popular blend, calling it 'Entire Butt' to signify that it was a single brew rather than a blend. The Blue Last was a popular watering hole among brawny market porters, and the rest is history.

Porter was the first beer to be brewed on an industrial scale, making it cheaper and more reliable, thus more popular among the British working classes. It came to dominate the beer market, fuelling the Industrial Revolution as surely as the coal in factory furnaces. And porter is as 'London' as jellied eels, despite its latter-day Irish associations.

Arthur Guinness, originally an ale brewer, unleashed his world-conquering Irish stout in 1759, using unmalted roasted barley for a drier flavour. The company was able to steal a march on London's brewers when the British government imposed restrictions on malting and beer strengths during the First World War. Stylish advertising and the canny appropriation of St Patrick's Day did the rest. Today, like IPA, porter is a resurgent style having been seized upon by American craft brewers looking for extremes of flavour.

Porter derives its typical espresso coffee and bitter chocolate flavours from dark-roasted malts. Although heavily hopped, it is best described as a malt-accented style, and it should be refreshing and quaffable, despite its dark, brooding demeanour.

So, what's the difference between porter and stout? These days, brewers have a somewhat fluid attitude towards labeling these dark beers, so that one man's stout is another man's porter. As a rule of thumb, however, porter is generally slightly sweeter than stout with a little less of the burnt flavours. Stout, or 'dry stout' as it is sometimes called, is theoretically drier, fuller-bodied and stronger in alcohol. Porter came first, with 'stout' an abbreviation of 'stout porter', which was actually a compliment in the olden days.

You will need to brush up on stout variations if you are to hold court convincingly. Yes, milk stout does contain lactose (milk sugars). These cannot be fermented into alcohol by ordinary ale yeast (Saccharomyces cerevisiae), leaving the finished beer both sweeter and less alcoholic, usually between 3% and 3.5%. Despite the claims of Mackeson, the first commercially brewed milk stout, that 'It looks good, tastes good and by golly it does you good', there is no evidence that stout is better for you than any other type of beer. It certainly contains no more iron, as was widely supposed. Still, milk stout is less gassy than other stouts, which is nice for the ladies.

Oyster stout is meant to contain real oysters, though many use granulated extract of bivalve, to add a hint of briny bitterness and some additional smoothness. Oatmeal stout contains additional malted or unmalted oats to give a smoother, slightly nuttier texture. Chocolate stout is made with additional chocolate malt and, occasionally, actual chunks of chocolate.

Imperial stout, sometimes known as Imperial Russian stout or Baltic porter, is a truly headbanging version which the late Saddam Hussein might have described as 'the Mother of all Stouts'. Immensely popular among Russia's 'The Great' family – that's Peter and Catherine – these tarry, treacly monsters were loaded with hops and alcohol (up to 10%) to survive rough North Sea crossings. Porter has remained popular in the Baltic States, Scandinavia and Eastern Europe to this day.

Stouts to shout about include Wye Valley's buxom

Dorothy Goodbody's Wholesome Stout (4.6%) from Herefordshire; Harveys dense and slightly sour Imperial Extra Double Stout (9%) from Sussex; Dark Star's lethally strong Imperial Stout (10.5%), also from Sussex; and North Coast Brewing's 'kick-ass' Old Rasputin (9%) from Fort Bragg, California. These latter two are made in the turbo-charged style that wowed the Russian court. Meantime London Porter (6.5%), meanwhile, introduces an element of wild yeast to recreate the slightly sour edge of the original eighteenth-century London style.

BITTER

'Bitter': it's not a word that would impress a modern-day focus group in search of a catchy brand name. In fact, it would be a marketing manager's worst nightmare. You won't see much of the 'B-word' on American beers, even on beers that are so bitter they'll melt your fillings. But to put 'bitter' into context, the name was coined in England, a country where aged styles of beer were traditionally described as 'stale'; a place that still delights in names like Old Jock Strap, Kilt Sniffer, Old Pondwater and The Dog's Bollocks (all real beer names).

To the uninitiated, bitter might not sound overly appetising but, as you know, bitterness is not always the overriding quality of bitter beers. Synonymous with the great British boozer, where it is still the default style of ale, bitter developed as a weaker version of pale ale; an expedient response to a shortage of raw materials during and immediately after the Second World War. While pale ale, and IPA in particular, can be intensely bitter as a consequence of heavy hopping, bitters, ironically, generally seek more of a balance between hoppy bitterness and malty sweetness. They are, however, more bitter than the sweeter, malt-forward style known as 'mild', which happened to be incredibly popular in the 1950s and 1960s when bitter rose to prominence. Like brownness, degrees of bitterness are relative, and the 'bitter' name arose to differentiate between this style and mild.

Bitter comes in three basic styles: 'ordinary', the weakest, at 3-4%; 'best' or 'special' at about 4.5-5%; and 'extra special' from 5.5-6%. The original 'extra special bitter' is the legendary Fuller's ESB, a 'marmalade and fruitcake' heavyweight at 5.5% from Fuller's Griffin brewery in West London. 'Ordinary' bitters are perfect 'session beers', in that you can sink a few without becoming too tired and emotional. Drink the same number of ESBs and you'll be telling the landlord's dog how much you love him.

Cult names to drop into conversation would include Harveys superbly balanced, hop-forward Sussex Best Bitter (4%), and the delightfully aromatic and fruity Timothy Taylor Landlord (4.3%), arguably Yorkshire's most famous beer (popularly known as either 'Tim Taylor' or, simply, 'Landlord'). Okay, so Timothy Taylor describes itself as a 'Strong Pale Ale', but it's won so many awards in the 'Best Bitter' category that you have to wonder.

MILD

What's so mild about mild? Returning to our theory of English beer relativity, as applied to shades of brownness and bitterness, it's less bitter than pale ale, porter and bitter. It's also less alcoholic than these beer styles, with the possible exception of some 'ordinary' bitters. But when it comes to depth of colour and flavour, mild is no slouch.

Nowadays, mild is fashionably retro among those in the know.

Typically, it's a malt-focused style with hops very much in the background, hence its rich, fruity palate with hints of caramel, coffee, chocolate and liquorice. Despite mild's relatively sweet palate, its low alcohol content (about 3-3.5%) renders it most refreshing, and it was prized by English factory workers as much for its quaffability as for its affordability. In the 1970s, mild's northern, cloth-cap image began to grate, especially among la-di-da southerners with their newfangled wines and aspirational lagers. Nowadays, of course, mild is fashionably retro among those in the know.

Go wild over Joseph Holt's Smooth Mild (3.2%), a dark, caramel-flavoured beer from Manchester; and misty-eyed over Moorhouse's absurdly smooth and satisfying Black Cat (3.4%) from Lancashire. Score further bluffing points by pointing out that Holt's Mild, with 32 bitterness units, is actually bitterer than some bitters. And browner.

GOLDEN ALE

Golden ales have been the golden boys of the British independent brewing scene for about the last 30 years. It's a relatively new ale style, heavy on the hops and light on malt, that cunningly combines the easy-drinking refreshment of lager with the depth and flavour of ale. What's not to like? Best served chilled, these are light- to medium-bodied ales using a biscuity, pale-malt springboard to show citrusy, floral hops at their bouncing best. Proving equally appealing to open-minded lager drinkers and dyed-in-the-wool real-ale types, golden ales have swept the boards at British beer festivals. Some commentators – and you can join them if you wish – argue that golden ales have almost single-handedly revived interest in craft brewing. We have, it seems, been mesmerised by gold.

Your favourites, of course, are the two beers that set the golden bandwagon rolling in the late 1980s. Sparkling Exmoor Gold (4.5%) from Somerset was intended as a one-off beer, brewed to celebrate an anniversary; while zingy, straw-coloured Summer Lightning (5%) from the Hop Back Brewery in Wiltshire was launched as a seasonal summer beer. Due to popular demand, however, both beers are now brewed all year round.

Like IPAs and pale ales, British golden ales have a marvelous affinity with the zesty, citrus flavours of American hops. Adnams Explorer (4.3%) from Suffolk, for example, is a light, refreshing golden ale brimming with grapefruity goodness from American Columbus and Chinook hops.

SCOTTISH ALE

Because hops don't grow in Scotland, brewers of traditional Scottish ales have tended, historically, to be quite frugal with their hops, concentrating instead on dark, malty, comforting brews.

Traditionally, Scottish ales are categorised according to an archaic system based on nineteenth-century barrel prices, which the aspiring bluffer would do well to learn. In ascending order of potency, we have '60 shilling', or 'light', ales with less than 3.5% ABV; '70 shilling', or 'heavy', ales with 3.5-4%; and '80/90 shilling', or 'export', ales ranging from 4-5.5%. '100 shilling' and upwards, also known as 'wee heavy', denotes a kilt-lifting 6-11% ABV. Obviously, richness and body intensify as we move up the scale. And do bear in mind that for some inexplicable reason 'Scottish ales' become 'Scotch ales' when they reach giddy 'wee heavy' levels.

Traditional Scottish ales are enjoying something of a revival in France, the USA and, in particular, Belgium, where Gordon Highland Scotch Ale, once imported, has been brewed since the 1960s. Apparently, the Belgians acquired a taste for the stuff from Scottish regiments stationed there during the First World War.

You may come across craft-brewed Scottish ales made with peat-smoked barley, presumably inspired by peat-smoked Scotch whisky. There is no tradition of peat-smoked barley in Scottish brewing, so regard it with the same suspicion you might reserve for a tin of shortbread with Japanese writing on the lid.

Pine for Auld Reekie over a pint of Belhaven 80 Shilling (4.2%). But please don't sing.

WELSH ALE

Hops don't grow to any significant extent in Wales either, although traditionally they were grown in the Cardiff area before Welsh breweries joined the wider British trend to import their hops from abroad. Interestingly, that's about to change with an intriguing 'guerilla gardening' project to grow the Prima Donna variety, which is particularly well suited to urban farming. DIY hop-growing packs have been distributed among enthusiasts across the city. The scheme, overseen by the Artisan Brewery in Pontcanna, Cardiff, is expected to result in an exclusively Cardiff craft beer, provisionally called 'Taff Temptress'.

Wales has been unjustly derided as something of a brewing backwater, but bluffers should be aware that there are more than 50 breweries (mostly of the micro persuasion) across the country. Per capita, extrapolated across both nations, this exceeds the number in England, effectively knocking the backwater allegation on its head. And, of course, England doesn't have the splendidly named 'Brains' brewery founded by Samuel Arthur Brain in 1882, probably best known for its flagship ale, Brains SA, a light-coloured bitter better known as 'Skull Attack'.

OLD ALE

How old is old? When it comes to beer and women the definition seems quite flexible, optional even. If it's labelled as 'old ale' you should expect a dark, warming, treacly experience similar to Scottish ale or barley wine, with flavours of dried fruit and molasses. It should also, ideally, have at least 6% ABV. But these days the 'old' adjective is bandied around quite freely and might mean anything from six months to a year. Sometimes it's slapped onto slightly beefed-up milds. You have been warned.

While there has never been a historical definition of what constitutes 'old ale', it is generally agreed that the style has mutated over the last 200 years. In the late eighteenth and early nineteenth centuries these beers were variously referred to as 'stock' ales, 'strong' ales or (the marketing man's dream) 'stale' ales. They contained very few hops, if any, and were mellowed by long ageing in wooden tuns, losing virtually all carbonation in the process. Exposure to wild yeasts over time would have given them a slightly sour edge with hints of soy sauce and Marmite (other yeast extracts are available). You must rue the passing of this slightly savoury style, but take heart from Theakston's Old Peculier (5.6%) from North Yorkshire with its old-time notes of sour fruit and balsamic vinegar.

Other old ales to get excited about include Gales Prize Old Ale (9%) from Fuller's; Greene King's Strong Suffolk Vintage Ale (6%); and Fuller's Vintage Ale (8.5%). First produced in 1997, Fuller's Vintage Ale is released each autumn, with the brewery hosting comparative tastings of each vintage. No doubt you've attended a few of these events, and heartily concur with the brewery's assessment that Fuller's Vintage Ale will mature 'well beyond the "best before" date' which they are obliged to state'.

Thomas Hardy's Ale is one to wax lyrical about and, of course, you are familiar with its history. It was created in 1968 by the now-defunct Eldridge Pope brewery to mark the 40th anniversary of Hardy's death. Production ceased in 1999, amidst much wailing and gnashing of teeth, only to be revived, using the same recipe, by O'Hanlon's brewery of Exeter in 2003. Point out that Thomas Hardy's Ale is probably Britain's strongest beer at 11.7%, and is purported to mature for up to 25 years in bottle. Contemplate the bottle in your hand while quoting Hardy's description of Dorchester strong beer, which inspired this brew: 'It was of the most beautiful colour that the eye of an artist in beer could desire; full in body, yet brisk as a volcano; piquant, yet without a twang; luminous as an autumn sunset; free from streakiness of taste, but, finally, rather heady.' Only the keenest observer would notice you're reading from the label.

BARLEY WINE

Anyone who fancies themselves as a bit of a beer expert, perhaps envious of your 'zymurlogical' prowess, might argue that Thomas Hardy's Ale is not an old ale but is, in fact, a barley wine. First, point out that zymurgy, the study of brewing, is analogical to metallurgy, liturgy and dramaturgy, so it should be zymurgical prowess. Then, giving them just enough rope, ask them to explain the difference between old ale and barley wine, because surely no one can. They both take a walk on the rich, malty side, they're both capable of maturing in bottle, and both are strong in alcohol.

The 'barley wine' name was coined in the eighteenth century during one of Britain's many contretemps with France. With wine hard to come by, it became every Englishman's patriotic duty to drink beer instead. Ultra-strong brews, aged in wood for a year or more, were created to take the place of wine at the Englishman's table. Indeed, The London and Country Brewer (1736) mentions very potent ales brewed 'as to be of a Vinous Nature'.

Mention that barley wine's strength (usually 6-12%) has earned it the ominous sobriquet 'stingo', and is the reason why it is traditionally served in 6oz 'nip' bottles. And confess to being an avid collector of JW Lees Harvest Ale (11.5%) from Manchester. Like Fuller's Vintage Ale, it is released every autumn in vintage-dated bottles, which you enjoy comparing with like-minded individuals.

Barley wine is enjoying a renaissance among the craft brewing fraternity, especially in the USA and Belgium, but they're not allowed to call it barley wine in the USA in case the 'wine' bit is misleading. To avoid confusion they must refer to it as 'barleywine-style ale'. You could also mention that brewers on America's West Coast are breaking with tradition by making heavily hopped 'barleywine-style ales' – no doubt because of the proximity of America's hop gardens in Oregon and Washington State, but people might think you're being pretentious. A good example would be Sierra Nevada's Bigfoot Barleywine Style Ale (9.6%), which tosses in Cascade, Centennial and Chinook hops, giving it complex bitter citrus notes.

Apparently, some US craft brewers release excessively strong barleywine-style ales just to show off at Christmas. Who would have thought it?

EIN STEIN (IS NOT ENOUGH)

HELLES

Taking its cue from the original golden Pilsner, created in Pilsen, Bohemia, in 1842, helles was first brewed at Munich's Spaten brewery in 1894, making it probably Germany's first golden lager. Also known as 'Munich original lager', helles is the everyday, go-to brew for Münchners in search of a good time. It's the fizzy Bavarian blonde that launched a thousand lederhosen; and still launches them nightly in Munich's heaving biergartens.

Hell means 'light', but don't let that fool you, as this really refers to the beer's colour. Helles is indeed a refined, quaffable thirst-quencher, but it can be quite full-bodied with plenty of malt and floral hop character. German golden lagers (hell, let's call them Pilsners) tend to have a drier, leaner and paler malt profile than their Bohemian brethren, leading to a more pronounced, assertive bitterness, don't you find?

At 5.2% ABV, Augustiner Helles is a brand that

Münchners hold dear. It's made in Munich's oldest, still-independent brewery, and is famous locally for its refusal to advertise. It is held aloft in brimming, swaying steins, not by a massive ad spend, but by the love of the locals.

MÄRZEN AND OKTOBERFESTBIER

In the days before refrigeration, Bavarian brewers would stockpile strong, heavily hopped beers in the spring and store them in cold caves and cellars through the hot summer months for autumn/winter drinking. Thus, these full-bodied, off-dry, malty beers were often brewed in March (*März*) and cracked open in October (*Oktober*) amid wild celebrations. This is how the world's biggest beer festival, Munich's Oktoberfest, was born. If you plan to attend, and hope to sound as if you know something about German beer, you'll need most of the information in this chapter.

Märzen and Oktoberfestbier derive their warm copper-red colours from amber malts, sometimes called 'Vienna malt' in reference to the off-dry, reddish beers once brewed in that city. This is yet another style enjoying a revival among US craft brewers. Hacker-Pschorr Oktoberfest Märzen (5.8%), balancing sweet, smooth maltiness with a touch of crisp hop bitterness, is a fine example of this seasonal session beer.

DUNKEL AND SCHWARZBIER

We've lumped dunkels and schwarzbiers together because they're both dark beers, but do not make the schoolboy error of confusing the two. *Dunkel* means 'dark' and is used as a prefix to describe a whole range of German beers. These are mostly lagers, but then most German beers are lagers. For example, you might also encounter a dunkel hefeweizen, a dark wheat beer, which is, of course, an ale. *Schwarzbier*, on the other hand, translates as 'black beer' and is, specifically, a style of lager. As a rule of thumb, schwarzbiers are darker than dunkels. But while they are blacker and more opaque, schwarzbiers also tend to be drier and lighter-bodied. Their easy-drinking style is not what you might expect from their inky colour scheme. Köstritzer Schwarzbier (4.8%) looks rather like a stout and is typical of the light schwarzbier style.

The best-known dunkel lager is Münchner dunkel which, before fancy-schmancy golden helles came knocking, was the everyday beer of Bavaria. Brewed traditionally from dark Munich malt, Münchner dunkel ranges from deep reddish mahogany to dark brown. It's a sweetish, malt-forward, hop-backward style with whiffs of toasted caramel. Soft, smooth Kaltenberg König Ludwig Dunkel (5.1%) is a mouthful in more ways than one, and is typical of the Münchner dunkel style. On no account confuse Münchner dunkel with dunkel hefeweizen or, indeed, Engelbert Humperdink.

You'll always score bluffing points, and admiring glances, with a dark lager in your hand.

BOCK

Savouring the rich malty depths of a dark, strong bock lager, you might like to reflect (aloud, obviously) on a rare example of punning on a German beer label. 'Bock' is a corrupted abbreviation of Einbeck, the town near Hanover where this style originated. But, apparently, if you say 'Einbeck' in a Bavarian accent it sounds like *ein bock,* which means 'billy goat'. 'Look,' you can point out, 'there's even a cute little goat on the label.' And the more bock you drink, the funnier it all gets. Those long winter evenings will just fly past.

♔

'Milk is for babies. When you grow up you have to drink beer.'

Arnold Schwarzenegger

The depiction of goats on bock labels serves as a warning; hovering between 6.3% and 7%, it's a headbanging lager with a kick like a mule (a butt like a goat doesn't sound quite right). 'Doppelbock', also known as *starkbier* ('strong beer'), is even more potent, climbing from 7% to the giddy heights of 14%.

First brewed in the fourteenth century, bock-style lagers were made and drunk by monks to provide sustenance through the fasting period of Lent, with the beers being referred to as 'liquid bread'. The first ever doppelbock was brewed by monks at the legendary Paulaner brewery in Munich. They called it Salvator ('Saviour') and trademarked the name in 1896. It proved so popular that rival breweries couldn't resist copying it, even adding the '-ator' suffix to their beers. This, you can explain, is why doppelbocks all over the world still have names like Detonator, Devastator and, our favourite, Smooth Hoperator from Pennsylvania. Every March in Munich, the Starkbierzeit festival ('strong beer time') marks the end of winter with the official tapping ('cracking open') of a cask of Paulaner Salvator.

Eisbock is a particularly strong version where the concentration is cranked up by freezing the beer. Because water freezes at a lower temperature than alcohol, it can be removed in the form of ice. Typically, the beer loses about 10% of its water and winds up with about 10% ABV. While most bocks are malty and sweetish, maibocks are relatively hoppy and bitter, at a similar strength to doppelbock. Strong wheat beers are known as weizenbocks.

Name-drop Paulaner Salvator (7.9%), obviously, and Weltenburger Kloster Asam Bock (6.9%) which tastes a bit like sweet brown bread; liquid bread, if you will.

RAUCHBIER

The golden rule of beer bluffing is never to show surprise when tasting a beer. If you let on that it's your first time, your cover will be blown. Thus, if some mischievous soul hands you a rauchbier, you must on no account skip about shouting, 'Oh my god, this tastes just like smoky bacon!' It's meant to.

Rauchbier, which means 'smoke beer', can be made in any style but is usually a dark, medium-strength lager.

Before the development of coke-fired kilns in the late eighteenth century, all malt was smoky to a greater or lesser degree. But while the rest of the brewing world adopted the new, cleaner malting methods, the brewers of Franconia in northern Bavaria resolutely continued to smoke their malt over beechwood fires. Today, this anachronistic oddity is a regional speciality. It's a love-it or hate-it style but, as a seasoned pro, you have no choice but to love it. The best-known rauchbier is Aecht Schlenkerla (5.1%) which tastes like smoked ham dipped in lapsang souchong. Forewarned is forearmed.

Observe that Upper Franconia has more breweries per square mile (roughly one per 19) than anywhere else in Europe and therefore, probably, the world.

GERMAN ALES

WEISSBIER/WEIZEN

Pale and interesting wheat beers may look vaguely lager-ish, but they are in fact ales (top-fermented), and they are not made exclusively from wheat. By law, German wheat beers must contain at least 50% wheat, though in practice most contain somewhere between 60% and 70%, the remainder being malted barley. Wheat, as you know, produces tarter, slightly edgier flavours than barley, and you can have too much of a good thing. But the main reason for not making pure, 100% wheat beers is purely practical. Because wheat has no husks, an all-wheat mash would be nearly impossible to 'lauter', i.e., separate the wort (sugar-rich solution, pre-fermentation) from spent grain. Basically, it's a bugger to fish all the bits out. German wheat beers tend to have higher wheat content, and therefore tend to be slightly more tart, than their Belgian counterparts.

It is socially acceptable to describe wheat beers as tasting of 'bubblegum'. In fact, it's the go-to description for anyone struggling with adjectives. Other typical descriptors include 'clove' and 'banana', which surely explains why wheat beers remain an acquired taste for some. You, of course, acquired it years ago. Been there, tasted that, got the T-shirt.

If you're going to wax lyrical about German wheat beers, you'll need to know your hefeweizen from your dunkelweizen. Throughout most of Germany, wheat beer is known as *weissbier,* which actually means 'white beer'. Only in Bavaria is it called *weizen* ('wheat'). The terms are largely interchangeable, though the weizen beers of the south might be a tad less tart. They are certainly less sharp than Berliner weisse, a Berlin speciality which is so 'refreshing' that the locals sometimes add an alleviating dash of raspberry or woodruff syrup to take the edge off it. Berliner weisse is exposed to lactobacillus bacteria (also used in Belgian lambics) which produces sour lactic acid flavours. The brand, Berliner Kindl Weisse (3%), is typical of this zippy, low-alcohol style.

Most wheat beer is packaged unfiltered, hence its cloudy appearance. In Germany these are called *hefeweizen* ('yeast wheat'), while *kristallweizen* are filtered and, therefore, crystal-clear. The clue's in the name. As you might expect, unfiltered hefeweizen are fuller-bodied with more pronounced bubblegum and banana flavours; kristallweizen are generally lighter and more refreshing for those less keen on Bazooka (other bubble gums are available).

For the record, the Bavarians also make dark wheat beers, dunkelweizen, and turbo-charged wheat beers called weizenbock.

When in Germany, do not ask for a slice of lemon or orange in your wheat beer as this is likely to offend. The oils in the pith destroy the head and mask delicate flavours. The Germans leave it to the Belgians to spruce up their witbiers with coriander, cumin and dried orange peel.

Ask for Schneider Weisse Unser Original (5.4%) if you're less keen on banana. Order hefty Schneider Weisse Unser Aventinus (8.2%), a weizenbock, if you want more bang for your buck.

KÖLSCH

Kölsch means 'from Köln', which is, of course, Cologne. Its appearance is pale and lager-like, even though it's made with top-fermenting yeast, so it is officially an ale. The trick, you see, is to use very pale malts and then store the beer for a long period at cool temperatures, as you would a lager. The result is a subtle, delicate brew with the lightness, freshness and fizz of lager, but with fruity ale overtones, at around 4.3-5%. You could say it's a distant relative of the golden/blonde British ale style, which is currently so popular.

Germans take great regional pride in their beers, so you won't be surprised to learn that kölsch accounts for more than half the beer drunk in Cologne. And because it's 'their beer', the people of Cologne have their own drinking rituals. Kölsch is traditionally served in small (20cl), straight-sided glasses called 'stange', much to the amusement of Münchners (from Munich) with their massive one-litre penis substitutes called steins. But maybe the kölsch drinkers have the last laugh as their beer, in its much smaller glass, never hangs around long enough to lose its cool.

Should you ever find yourself in an *ausschank* ('brewery tap') in downtown Cologne, you will be served by blue-clad waiters, referred to as 'Kobes', which is short for Jacob. Do not be alarmed. They patrol the aisles with trays of freshly poured kölsch, replacing glasses the moment they are empty and marking the sale on a coaster underneath your glass. When you know you've had enough (always difficult), simply place the coaster on top of your glass and the waiter will tally up the marks and present you with the bill. Very simple and very civilized. You might want to share this anecdote the next time you're waving a tenner at the bar of a heaving pub with elbows jabbing your kidneys.

Name-drop the hugely popular Dom Kölsch (4.8%) as the brand you drank in Cologne. Perhaps you preferred it because it contains a smidgen of wheat malt, but that's really up to you.

ALT

With hoppy overtones and richer malt flavours, the alt, or 'old', ales of Düsseldorf are the closest you will find in Germany to English-style ales. Like their Anglo-Saxon cousins, they're made with darker malts and top-fermenting ale yeasts but, like kölsch, receive a long, cool conditioning period typical of lager. Thus, you might wish to describe altbier as a hybrid beer. Deep copper-coloured Zum Uerige Alt (4.7%), with its complex, rounded caramel flavours and thick beige head, is typical of the style. It's been suggested that it's called 'old beer' because it predates the arrival of bottom-fermenting, golden lagers in Germany. It's certainly the only beer to be seen drinking in Düsseldorf's Altstadt ('old town'). Bluffers should not countenance any alternative.

CZECH IT OUT

As a pipe-smoking, corduroy-clad beer scholar, you are, of course, au fait with the enormous significance of the year 1842. This was the year in which a happy confluence of events gave birth to golden lager. From 9000 BC when the Mesopotamians first cracked the brewing code, right up until this annus mirabilis, all beer had been dark or cloudy, or both. With the gift of hindsight, now that golden lager accounts for some 80% of all beers drunk in the world, it is easy to appreciate the magnitude of this discovery.

If this lager landmark is the beer world's equivalent of the Nativity, the 'manger' was located in the Bohemian town of Pilsen, now in the Czech Republic. The good burghers of Pilsen had become so disillusioned with the quality of the town's beer that in 1839 they emptied barrels of the offending brew in front of the town hall. Vowing to brew a beer that would last longer and taste better, they began building the Bürgerliches Brauhaus (citizens' brewery), and appointed a Bavarian, Josef Groll, as brewmaster. Obviously a very talented brewer, Groll found himself in the right place at the right time.

The Czech Republic, or Bohemia as it was then, is blessed with brewing resources: some of the softest water in Europe and top-grade barley from the Hana plateau, seasoned with the highly prized Saaz hop from the north-western region of Zatec. Groll brought these together with cool-fermenting yeast from Bavaria and new malting techniques developed in England for producing pale ales. Bohemia's soft water extracted little colour from these newfangled pale malts to produce lager with a lightness and brightness that was hitherto unknown – golden even.

The process was aided by new cooling-coil technology, also from England, which enabled far greater control of the fermentation temperature, and by a vast network of cool sandstone cellars for long, leisurely, cold maturation.

The final piece of the serendipitous jigsaw was the simultaneous emergence of glass drinking vessels, known today as 'glasses'. What better material to show off this new golden beer in all its sparkling splendour? The effect would have been somewhat lost in the wooden and pewter mugs that glass eventually replaced.

Soon everyone was at it, with the Spaten brewery in Munich making its first golden lager in 1894. It was called 'helles' (again, 'hell' being the German for…'light' or 'clear'. Keep up at the back!). German immigrants wasted no time in taking golden lager across the Atlantic to America. The lager that laid the golden egg had bolted, long before anyone in Pilsen thought it might be a good idea to register the name 'Pilsner'.

As far as the bluffer is concerned, the only 'true' Pilsners (i.e. from Pilsen) are Pilsner Urquell and Gambrinus. Pilsner Urquell thought to add the 'Urquell' bit (meaning 'original source') in 1898 but this was woefully little, far too late.

'A fine beer may be judged with only one sip, but it's better to be thoroughly sure.'

Czech Proverb

Budweiser Budvar from the Bohemian city of České Budějovice may be considered an honorary Pilsner. Way back in the fifteenth century, the city was the site of the Royal Court brewery of Bohemia, which is how the city's beers came to be known as 'budweisers', meaning 'beer of kings'. Sadly, this name wasn't trademarked either, much to the delight of US brewing behemoth, Anheuser-Busch. Please note, you must never ever mistake Budweiser Budvar from the Czech Republic with American Budweiser. Remember the 'Budvar' bit and you'll be fine, unless you're in the USA. There, after more than 100 years of wrangling, and nearly as many lawsuits, Budweiser Budvar is called Czechvar.

To look as if you really know what you're talking about, reminisce about the time you drank Pilsner Urquell Kvasnicový in a tiny cellar bar in Pilsen. It's the unpasteurised, unfiltered version, hence slightly hazy, which seldom ventures beyond the city itself. Proper beer experts will doff their cloth caps in respect.

Over the years, as Pilsner-style lagers have spread around the globe, the once proud name has often been shortened to 'pils'. You can comment that it's not just the name that's been reduced, but the beer itself. The 'pils' name has been cheapened by thousands of 'fighting lagers' where malted barley is supplemented by maize, rice and syrups, while maturation time has been slashed to a couple of weeks. No corner has been left uncut in the pursuit of profit.

BELGO BEER

LAMBICS

Lambic beers are the ultimate in acquired taste, making them the bluffer's brew par excellence. While most brewers seek to balance malty sweetness with the bitterness and astringency of hops, lambic brewers take an alternative route, using heightened acidity to create balance. Thus, an appreciation of the dry, wine-like, cidery flavours of lambic beers – commonly described as 'old bookshop', 'hay barn' and 'horse blanket' – is something to which lesser beer drinkers can only aspire. Or to put it another way, lambics are for those perverse creatures who enjoy their beer flat and sour.

A niche product, which is seldom exported, lambic beer is made only in the Payottenland region just to the south-west of Brussels. And because lambics are made using local wild yeasts and bacteria, this is the closest the beer world gets to the wine concept of 'terroir' (a unique expression of a specific place). There are some who think the 'lambic' name is derived from the small town of Lembeek in Payottenland, and others, plainly bonkers, who think it isn't.

Lambics are feral beers made by a process called 'spontaneous fermentation', which is how all beers were made in the olden days. Rather than using cultivated yeast strains kept in hermetically sealed yeast banks, lambic brewers employ the services of wild, airborne yeasts and bacteria. Windows are left open to invite the little beasties in, while dust and cobwebs in the cellars are left undisturbed to preserve the unique microscopic critters that live there. This is not the sanitised school of beer making.

After a lengthy boil, the wort (baby beer) is left to cool in open, shallow tanks, where the wild yeasts have their wicked way. These Brettanomyces bruxellensis and Brettanomyces lambicus yeasts impart the trademark 'horse blanket' flavours, which those in the know abbreviate to 'Brett' – as in, 'Is it just me, or is there a touch of Brett to this beer?' Practice this at home in front of a mirror before trying it on your friends.

Once the beers are put in barrels, Brett stands aside and 'Lacto' (that's lactobacillus bacteria) takes over. While yeasts convert sugar into alcohol, lactobacillus bacteria convert sugar into lactic acid, producing the cidery, wine-like qualities for which lambics are renowned. Comment that, while most brewers go to enormous lengths to keep lactobacillus at bay, brewers of lambic beers and traditional Berliner weisse (wheat beer) actively encourage it.

Lambic brewers use plenty of hops, but only when they're old and oxidised (the hops, not the brewers), having lost their bittering qualities. They're used instead for their preservative properties, as lambic beers are often aged for up to three years. The grist (cereal mix) for lambics usually comprises 30-40% unmalted wheat, the remainder being malted barley. Lambic brewers to name-drop include De Troch, Girardin, Timmermans, Lindemans, Belle-Vue, Boon and Cantillon.

Lambics are seldom bottled neat, so to speak, and are generally sold on tap in Belgium's beer cafés. Of course, the De Rare Vos bar in Schepdaal is one of your regular haunts when visiting Payottenland.

Faro is a traditional draught beer, made by adding some brown sugar to a lambic brew. This sparks another fermentation, softening the acidity somewhat. But these days, faro is going the way of the dodo, so most lambic beers are transformed into more palatable gueuze and various fruit beers instead.

GUEUZE

One way to knock off some of lambic beer's sharp edges is to blend young and old lambics together to make gueuze. Youthful, zesty lambics of six to 12 months are blended with deeper-flavoured, wine-like lambics that have been matured in oak for two or three years. The blend, normally a ratio of one-third young lambic to two-thirds old, is bottled with a dash of sugar to provoke another fermentation (i.e., bottle-conditioned). Highly prized by connoisseurs like yourself, gueuze, with its Champagne-style bottle and wired cork, is sometimes referred to as 'Brussels Champagne'. It's certainly dry and sparkling like Champagne, and less tart than straight, unblended lambic beer.

Gueuze is pronounced 'gur-zah', 'kurrs' or even 'goose', depending on who you listen to. That's one of the interesting things about a country that speaks French, Flemish, Dutch and German. So take your pick. Get excited about Cantillon Gueuze (5%) with its sour green apple flavours.

KRIEK AND FRAMBOZEN (FRUIT BEERS)

An eye-catching glass of reddish fruit beer will mark you out as a discerning drinker in any bar, but make sure you're seen holding the right one. In recent years there's been a wave of ersatz gimmicky 'fruit beers' ranging from apple and apricot to pineapple and banana, mostly made with a squirt of fruit juice, syrup or purée. Do the right thing and choose *kriek* ('cherry') or *frambozen* ('raspberry') beers from Belgium, as these are the real deal. You're on even safer ground if your kriek is prefaced with the word *oude* ('old'), denoting that the base beer is lambic to which whole, fresh fruit has been added. It will taste remarkably dry and refreshing with an expertly poised sweet/sour balance; in other words 'grown-up' and not like something from the pick 'n' mix counter.

At the dawn of brewing, and long before hops were established as the brewer's seasoning of choice, a cornucopia of fruits, herbs and spices were used to alleviate the sweetness of malt-heavy brews. Juniper berries, rose hips, ginger, rosemary and bog myrtle have all been used, but the brewers of Belgium settled on cherries and raspberries. Kriek (cherry) beer is the most popular.

Oude kriek is made by steeping whole or crushed cherries in a cask of lambic for about six months. This provokes a vigorous fermentation, with the cask often overflowing with foam as the yeast devours the fruit. After cask maturation, the beer is then re-fermented in bottle. Traditionally, brewers used the very sour Schaarbeek cherry variety from the village of the same name on the outskirts of Brussels. You, of course, prefer it when they use whole cherries because the stones add a delicious hint of almond to the finished beer.

Today, the best-known brands are Liefmans, which uses Flemish brown ale as the base beer, macerated with whole fruit; and Lindemans, which adds fruit pulp to a lambic base beer. Get especially excited about the superbly balanced Boon Oude Kriek (6.5%).

TRAPPIST ALES

Made by monks, test-driven by robots, drunk by you. Okay, we made up the middle bit, but Trappist ales are indeed made by Trappist monks of the Order of Cistercians the Strict Observance. And you, naturally, are a connoisseur. Most beer nerds will tell you there are seven monasteries making Trappist ale, listing six in Belgium and one in the Netherlands. But you know better. The six Belgian monasteries, with the names of their beers in brackets, are Holy Heart of Westmalle (Westmalle), Our Lady of Scourmont (Chimay), Saint-Rémy (Rochefort), St Benedictus (Achel), St Sixtus (Westvleteren) and Orval (Orval), so good they named it twice. The Dutch Trappist monastery is De Koningshoeven, which makes La Trappe. You, however, can trump this list by adding the Stift Engelszell monastery in Austria, which makes Gregorius ale and earned its 'Authentic Trappist Product' badge as recently as October 2012.

Genuine Trappist ales are marked with this hexagonal 'Authentic Trappist' logo to differentiate themselves from common-or-garden Abbey beers (*see* below), and the distinction is important. The badge shows not only that the beer was brewed within the walls of a Trappist monastery, but also that profits are primarily intended to fund the monastic community and various charitable works, which is seldom the case with Abbey beers.

You should also be aware that 'Trappist' does not denote a single style of beer but rather a broad church of styles (do you see what we did there?) from bubbly blondes to dark sipping beers. What all Trappist beers do have in common is their potency, ranging from 6.5% ABV up to a cassock-busting 11.3%, and they are all unfiltered and unpasteurised. And, being top-fermented brews, they are all ales as opposed to lagers.

There are three principal styles of Trappist ale: Dubbel, which is a deep reddish brown with dried fruit and Christmas-cake flavours at about 6-7%; Tripel, which is golden and glorious with bitter marmalade and citrus flavours, ranging from 8-10%; and Quadrupel, which is a dark, sweet sipping beer with vinous, Madeira-like notes and strong enough to blow the roof off a cathedral.

Like some of the bock beers of Germany, Trappist ales

are traditionally consumed as 'liquid bread', to provide sustenance through the fasting period of Lent. But this doesn't mean the monks end up singing 'Roll Out the Barrel' and playing Twister for Easter eggs. For Trappists, drinking is not a sin but drunkenness is, so while the strong beers are sold off to fund the monastic lifestyle and various good deeds, the brewing brotherhood generally sticks to much weaker beers (about 3.5%) called Patersbier (Father's beer) or Enkel (single). Examples of these more angelic ales include Petite Orval and Chimay Dorée.

The Trappist monasteries developed their beers independently of each other, so they don't all label their beers as Dubbel, Tripel or Quadrupel. Chimay, for example, colour codes its different strengths, its Red, White and Blue labels corresponding with 7%, 8% and 9% ABV respectively. Rochefort, on the other hand, has gone for a numerical system, its Rochefort 6, 8 and 10 weighing in at 7.5%, 9.2% and 11.3% ABV. If anyone asks why the numbers don't correlate exactly with the alcoholic strengths, mumble something about the chosen numbers loosely referring to the amount of malt with fermentable sugars and the original gravity of the wort prior to fermentation. If they won't go away, mumble some more.

Perhaps the Trappist ale to get most excited about is Westmalle Tripel (9.5%), on the grounds that the Westmalle monastery created the Tripel style in 1934, making this the definitive version. It has a heavenly golden glow with earthy aromas and is packed with bitter-sweet citrus flavours with notes of aniseed. As with most other Trappist ales, 'complex' doesn't begin to do it justice, but rest assured that Westmalle Tripel is often touted as probably the best beer in the world. Carlsberg take note.

If you are ever presented with a Trappist ale from Westvleteren be sure to appreciate, and comment on, how hard it is to get hold of any. It can be bought only by phoning the abbey at specific times then buying a small allowance of what's available, for personal consumption only. It's as hard to acquire as the Holy Grail, which would, in fact, be the ideal vessel to drink it from. Speaking of which, each of the monasteries sells its own 'branded' chalice-/goblet-shaped glass for its beer. They are satisfyingly weighty and mould to the drinker's hand, elevating the enjoyment of these meditative ales to the transcendental. You, of course, own the full set.

ABBEY BEERS

This is a definition so loose as to be almost useless, but that doesn't mean you won't see 'Bière d'Abbaye' or 'Abdijbier' on countless Belgian beer labels. Neither term is any guarantee that the beer has been made even within chanting distance of an abbey. Some are made under a licensing agreement that benefits a named religious institution; others are named after fictitious or long-defunct abbeys, and have no ecclesiastical connections beyond a shifty-looking monk on the label. Indeed, up until a court ruling in 1962, some of the less scrupulous brewers even labelled their beers as 'Trappist'. In 1997 the International Trappist Association introduced its 'Authentic Trappist Product' label to remove any vestiges of doubt, stamping out this monky business once and for all.

Today, you can take 'Abbey beer' to mean that it's made in a vaguely Trappist style (*see* above). Consequently, you might come across Abbey beers labelled as Dubbel (dark with caramelised flavours) or Tripel (golden with bitter-sweet citrus flavours), or simply as Blonde or Brown (dark or light). Like Trappist ales, you can expect Abbey beers to be strong, top-fermented ales, generally somewhere between 6% and 9.5%. Unlike Trappist ales, which are bottle-conditioned, Abbey beers might be filtered.

Don't make the mistake of assuming that all Abbey beers are necessarily inferior to Trappist ales, as some have as much history and complexity with perhaps a touch more accessibility and drinkability about them. Grimbergen, for example, is an excellent range of beers, brewed by Heineken for Grimbergen Abbey just north of Brussels. The best-known Abbey beer is probably Leffe, now brewed by global brewing giant AB InBev at a large Stella Artois facility in Leuven, but still paying royalties to Abbaye Notre-Dame de Leffe where it originated in the thirteenth century.

FLANDERS BROWN AND RED ALES

Flanders Brown and Red ales are distantly related cousins from East and West Flanders respectively. Family traits include sweet fruity aromas, often cherry and plum, combined with a refreshing, almost wine-like sourness on the finish.

Hailing from the East Flanders town of Oudenaarde, Flanders Brown ales derive their astringency from lengthy ageing in oak barrels crawling with wild yeasts and lactobacillus bacteria. It's because of this extended ageing that this style is often referred to as 'Old Brown', or 'Oud Bruin' to the initiated. Traditionally, younger beers are blended with older beers to round off some of the sharper edges, giving Brown ales a slightly maltier, caramelised quality.

West Flanders Red ales, made with a special reddish malt, tend to have a touch more of the 'barnyard' qualities associated with wild Brettanomyces yeast, so it never hurts to draw attention to a touch of 'Brett yeast' when tasting them.

Wax lyrical about the richness and wine-like complexity of Liefmans Goudenband Brown ale (8%). When it comes to the Red corner, you're a huge fan of copper-coloured Rodenbach (5.2%) with its lively sweet 'n' sour charms.

SAISON AND BIÈRE DE GARDE

Belgian Saison and French Bière de Garde (which is close enough to pass as Belgian) are often lumped together in an unwieldy category called 'Farmhouse ales'. It refers to a tradition of agrarian brewing in the French region of Nord-Pas de Calais and in French-speaking Wallonia in southern Belgium. Back in the day these beers were made with anything that came to hand on a farm – barley, wheat and rye, both malted and unmalted, seasoned with a smorgasbord of herbs, spices and hops. Today, this equates with a random collection of styles with nothing in common bar their rural heritage. This very elusiveness, however, appeals to experimentally minded craft brewers both in Europe and the USA, who choose to label some of their funkier brews as Saison, Bière de Garde or Farmhouse ale (describe any flavours you can't quite pinpoint as 'funky', but bear in mind that the word does have farmyardy connotations). Stylistically, these beers are as hard to nail as jelly to a ceiling, but that doesn't excuse the bluffer from having an opinion. In fact, that should be your opinion.

'They who drink beer will think beer'.

Washington Irving

Anyway, it all started down on the farm in the days before refrigeration. Because it was impossible to control fermentation in the hot summer months, the brewing season traditionally ran from late autumn to early spring in order to lay down a supply of beer for later in the year. This rather suited the rural community, as it provided additional winter employment on one hand, and spent grains for feeding livestock on the other. Fresh, relatively low-alcohol beers (typically, around 3 to 4%) were made to hydrate farm hands at harvest time. Bigger brews (up to 8%) would be stored for 'refreshment' later in the year, the higher alcohol helping to prevent spoilage. *Bière de Garde* translates as 'beer for keeping' (obvious, really) and it was sometimes 'kept' in Champagne-style bottles with wired corks, the Champagne region being not very far away. Saison is so-called because it was the drink of 'saisonniers', migrant workers who came to help with the harvest.

We can't be sure what early Farmhouse ales tasted like – L'industrie de la Brasserie, published in 1880, describes the Bière de Garde de Lille as being quite sour with a 'very vinous flavour' – but we can be sure that they have evolved to suit modern palates. While the originals were bottle-conditioned and top-fermented for rounder, fruitier flavours, there has been a creeping tendency towards filtering and bottom-fermenting to achieve cleaner, crisper, lager-style qualities.

If you must say anything, suggest that classic Bière de Garde is generally amber-coloured and malt-accented, with hops in the background, while Saisons are typically a tad drier, lighter in colour and with a shade more hoppy bitterness. However, there are so many exceptions that, before you know it, you'll be looking around for hammer, nails, jelly and a ladder.

All is not lost, however. For bluffing purposes you need to know only two beers which are now widely acknowledged as the archetypal examples of these two 'styles'. Cite Jenlain Ambrée (7.5%) from Brasserie Duyck as the benchmark Bière de Garde. First bottled in the 1940s, it was revamped in the 1950s when the alcohol content was doubled and it was packaged in recycled Champagne bottles, complete with wired cork. It achieved cult status among bolshy French students in the 1970s. Describe it as amber coloured, smooth and fruity with sweet, malty, barley-sugar flavours and spicy, liquorice notes, set off by a dry, bittersweet finish; unpasteurised, of course.

The classic Saison beer is Saison Dupont (6.5%), which, thanks to sterling work by its US importer, achieved cult status stateside in the 1980s. First brewed in 1844, this is a beautifully balanced copper-coloured ale with a billowing head, crusty-bread aroma, fruity apricot and citrus qualities, strong bitterness and a long, dry finish. Don't be caught out by its slight cloudiness as it's bottled unfiltered, and feel free to call it 'funky'.

And, yes, there really is a beer called Silly Saison, brewed by Brasserie Silly in the village of the same name.

WITBIER

First off, Belgian wheat beer is actually called white beer, which is *witbier* in Flemish and *bière blanche* in French. This refers to its unfiltered cloudy 'whiteness', which is really a pale lemony gold. Not white at all. Oh well.

Step one for the beer bluffer is to know the main differences between Belgian and German wheat beers. The Germans use a much higher proportion of wheat in the mash, somewhere between 50 and 70%, the remainder being malted barley, and the wheat is always malted. In Belgian brews, wheat usually accounts for about 30 to 40% of the mash, some of which might be unmalted. They might also contain a proportion of oats and spelt.

Belgian wheat beers tend to be lower in alcohol, at around 4.5-5%, and local Belgian yeast strains tend to be less aggressive in aroma and flavour than their German counterparts. Despite this, Belgian wheat beers tend to be spicier. The Germans would never 'adulterate' their wheat beers with the addition of spices, but the Belgians have no qualms about adding coriander, cumin and dried orange peel to the brew; these are the three most commonly used. Observe that dried peel from the Curaçao orange, as used in Hoegaarden, is a particularly bitter and most effective foil to the sweetness of malt. Also mention that wheat is excellent for 'head retention', as you wipe away your fetching foam moustache.

In the early 1900s, witbier began a serious decline, with many breweries ceasing production as golden lager soared in popularity. But in the mid-1960s, in the town of Hoegaarden, Belgian witbier began a remarkable comeback thanks to the efforts of one man. Pierre Celis died in 2011 but he is fondly remembered in brewing folklore as the single-minded saviour of the classic witbier style. A milkman by trade, Celis had worked for a spell at the Tomsin brewery, Hoegaarden's last producer of witbier, which closed its doors in 1957. In 1966, driven by what must have been one hell of a hankering for a pint, Celis set up his own brewery to pick up where Tomsin had left off. He brewed witbier, flavoured with cumin and dried Curaçao orange peel, which he named Oud Hoegaards. By the time its name had morphed into Hoegaarden, Celis's witbier had inspired a generation of brewers to pick up their mash forks and follow in his spicy footsteps. It's a life-affirming story of the lengths a man will go to for a pint of his favourite beer.

A lifelong devotee of Hoegaarden (which you know to pronounce as 'who-garden'), you are particularly keen on Hoegaarden Grand Cru. With ABV ranging from 8 to 10%, grand cru witbiers are fuller-bodied, more intense versions of common-or-garden witbiers. Hoegaarden Grand Cru weighs in at 8.5% with aromas of cloves and spices, and a racy citrus palate with hints of white chocolate.

The success of Blue Moon Belgian White (5.4%) from US brewing giant MillerCoors has raised the profile of witbiers in the USA. It's an unfiltered 'Belgo-American-style' white beer, spiced with orange peel and coriander and brewed with a proportion of oats for creaminess. Perhaps taking a cue from the ubiquitous lemon wedge stuffed into necks of Corona beer bottles, MillerCoors has promoted the serving of Blue Moon with a slice of orange in the glass. They would frown on this sort of thing in Belgium, but bars in the Netherlands have taken to providing muddlers to crush the fruit in the glass for an even greater citrusy punch. This raises the difficult question: where do you stand on a slice of orange?

'Mmm…beer.'

Homer Simpson

CRAFT BEERS:
AN AMERICAN REVOLUTION

Should you ever find yourself cornered in a snug bar by a flatulent beery-breathed bore looking accusingly at the 'Euro-fizz' in your glass, do not panic. Even as he drones on about original gravity and International Bittering Units, his beard flecked with foam and pork-scratching detritus, you will be able to hold your own if you show passable knowledge of the brewing revolution that's sweeping through the world of beer. Your opening gambit is that you are, in fact, drinking a potent American-style Pilsner based on an authentic Bohemian recipe. Then, while he's still reeling, deliver a swift uppercut: 'It seems as though the brewing world might be in the early throes of an American century – or half-century, at least. Don't you agree?'

REVOLUTION OR EVOLUTION?

After decades of dumbing down and global domination by a handful of behemoth brands, beer is getting its mojo back, especially in terms of flavour and variety. You could back-pedal a little bit by conceding that it might be more of a renaissance rather than a full-blooded revolution, seeing as the new wave of small craft breweries are delving into beer's heritage in order to move forward. It's a revivalist trend, with passionate, artisan brewers reinterpreting the classic European beer styles, albeit with a modern twist, and, in the process, reintroducing the F-word (flavour). Some are fermenting with wild yeasts, experimenting with barrel ageing and seasoning their beers with all manner of fruits, herbs and spices, but these are time-honoured techniques. What's really changing is the business model and philosophy.

THE RISE OF THE GIANTS

Small breweries were poleaxed by Prohibition in the USA in the 1930s, and annihilated by the First and Second World Wars in Europe. This cleared the way for the rise of multinational brewing giants, answerable to their shareholders and run by accountants. In broad terms, the tendency was to commoditise beer in the pursuit of profit. Some accelerated the brewing process by reducing fermentation and conditioning times. Costs were also cut by supplementing the sugars from malted barley with cheap adjuncts (alternative sources of fermentable sugars) such as maize, rice, starch and even liquid sugar. Contributing neither the body nor complexity derived from malted barley, these budget-priced alternatives can account for as much as one-third of fermentable sugars in 'industrial' beers. So far, so bad.

Some of these beers are then filtered and pasteurised to

within an inch of their lives in the name of cost-effective refreshment delivery. And now 'light' beers have evolved into 'ice' beers where any residue of flavour is cold-filtered and centrifuged away. Consequently, the world is awash with indistinguishable beers, as favoured by Homer Simpson; cheap, similar in taste and advertised everywhere.

Indeed, with global marketing departments more concerned with building brand loyalty than offering anything 'challenging', we do, to an extent, drink their advertising. Our expectations fell as the beer market became increasingly homogenised, reaching a beer nadir in the 1970s and 1980s. The bland were leading the blind.

THE REBIRTH OF BEER

But lo! What light through yonder (pub) window breaks? In these organic, eco-friendly, touchy-feely Twenty-tens, we've reconnected with our consumer conscience, fretting about food miles and actually reading labels. Whether our rediscovered interest in the quality and provenance of beer has been fuelled by the spread of craft brewing, or vice versa, is as hard to answer as the Chicken McNugget and Egg McMuffin conundrum, but now there is no putting the genie back in the bottle.

The epicentre of the craft brewing movement was in northern California, where they began by reinventing European beers, 'American-style'. Essentially, they made amplified versions of the classics with various elements cranked up to 11. American-style English IPAs, for example, raised bitterness to unprecedented levels, using aggressively pungent American hops like Cascade, Centennial and Chinook, while American 'barleywine-styles' and Imperial porters ramped up the alcohol by several decibels. These are beers not to be messed with, and they have inspired a whole new generation of craft brewers around the world.

Of course, it's now gone full circle with brewers in Britain and Belgium, for example, rejigging these American reinventions, sometimes using American hops, and exporting them back to America in a virtuous circle of mutual admiration and cross-fertilisation of ideas.

The long and the short of it is that adventurous beer drinkers have never had it so good, and the styles that you've painstakingly genned up on using this book – from alt, helles and dunkel to saison, lambics and witbier – are now appearing even in supermarkets beyond their native shores.

BEWARE STEALTH BEERS

The huge global brands are seeing their traditional markets being slowly nibbled away and are turning their attention to new markets like China and India, where these pesky artisan beers have yet to make any impression. Some of the big boys have even resorted to making their own cunningly disguised 'craft beers', referred to by those in the know as 'stealth beers'. Indeed, the craft beer movement is gradually becoming the tail that's wagging the dog.

SMALL IS BEAUTIFUL

Here are some statistics for you to wheel out like a mighty medieval siege machine, should the occasion demand it. According to the Brewers Association in the USA, in 2010 the country had 43 'non-craft' (i.e., 'big') brewing companies, making 166.5 million barrels of beer, with a market share of 82%. There were 1,716 craft brewers and brewpubs, making 9.95 million barrels, with a market share nudging 5%, the remainder being imports. What is significant is that the craft beer market saw gains in excess of 10%. In the late 1970s the USA had less than 50 brewing companies; today it has more than 1,800 breweries, most of them small and beautiful.

NAMING NAMES

To appear as if you really know what you're talking about, you're going to need some names and places. Cite John 'Jack' McAuliffe, who in 1976 founded the New Albion Brewing Company in Sonoma in northern California, as the original pioneer of the American craft beer movement. Drawing his inspiration from the breadth of beer styles he had encountered during his military service in Scotland, McAuliffe built a cult following. But New Albion wasn't big enough to withstand larger market forces and closed after six years. It was, however, the first microbrewery to open in the USA since Prohibition and a huge source of inspiration for those that followed. It is arguably the most important 'failed' brewery in history.

Another founding father is FL 'Fritz' Maytag, heir to a successful household appliance company, who bought a failing brewery in San Francisco in 1965. Dismayed that his favourite brewery was on the verge of bankruptcy, he 'did a Victor Kiam' and bought the Anchor Brewing Company. Its unique Anchor Steam Beer is still going strong.

BEERVANA

The revolution started in California but it has thrived and flourished in the Pacific Northwest, the region which happens to grow some 75% of American hops in the Yakima Valley in Washington and the Willamette Valley in Oregon. Portland, Oregon, alternatively known as 'Beervana' or 'Munich on the Willamette', has assumed the role of unofficial craft brewing capital of America. It has more craft breweries and brewpubs than any other US city and hosts one of the country's most important beer events, the Oregon Brewers Festival, at the end of July. In fact, craft beers account for nearly half of all beers drunk in Portland, compared with a national figure of about 5%.

THE WIDER PICTURE

Pepper any discussion of the US craft brewing scene with the names of some of the more prominent breweries: Sierra Nevada Brewing Company in Chico, California; Goose Island in Chicago; Great Divide in Denver, Colorado; Brooklyn Brewery, New York; Dogfish Head in Milton, Delaware; New Belgium Brewing Company in Fort Collins, Colorado; The Boston Beer Company and the Harpoon Brewery, both in Boston; and Deschutes Brewery in beautiful Bend, Oregon, whose motto is, 'The meek shall inherit, well, some pretty dull beers'.

Brewpubs are, as they sound, restaurants with craft

breweries attached. By selling direct to the public, these have played a vital role in the spread of the movement, and some of the big brewers, like Delaware's Dogfish Head, started out as brewpubs. Name-drop the following, who were the biggest brewpubs in 2010: Hopworks Urban Brewery and Laurelwood Brewing Company, both in Portland; Elysian Brewing Company in Seattle; Nodding Head in Philadelphia; and Tampa Bay Brewing Company in Florida.

The American backlash against boring beer has come a long way since the first beer was brewed in anger back in the 1970s. At the last count, there were no fewer than 75 categories at the Great American Beer Festival, the mecca of the craft beer movement held in Denver, Colorado. These included Bohemian-style Pilsner, Munich-style helles and American-style sour ale (based on the Belgian sour style). In a market still dominated by Bud and Coors Light, these are the beers beating at the gates.

BACK IN BLIGHTY

Meanwhile in the UK, it is said you are never more than 10 miles from a microbrewery, wherever you happen to be. This does make them sound rather like rats, but if microbreweries really are breeding like vermin, this is surely no bad thing. At the last count there were 500 microbreweries in the UK, some 90% of which, significantly, have been set up since 1990. According to SIBA (Society of Independent Brewers), the local brewing industry is the only segment of the UK beer market that's growing; and this growth has undoubtedly been stimulated by the introduction in 2002 of Progressive Beer Duty (or 'PBD', as you like to call it). Under this system, breweries pay tax according to their production levels, meaning that some microbreweries pay about half the standard duty rate.

You will notice that, with typical British reserve, small operators are still generally referred to as 'micro' rather than 'craft' breweries, though the Brits are slowly adopting the less diminutive American term. Actually, they also started out as 'microbreweries' in the USA, though the expression was always going to be short-lived in a country where you would never question the size of a Texan's mashfork.

THE CAMRA EFFECT

As in the USA, the winds of change started blowing in the UK in the 1970s. The first gust arrived in 1971 with the formation of CAMRA (Campaign for Real Ale), the original consumer pressure group with bland beer in its sights. You, of course, are aware that it was originally known as the Campaign for the Revitalisation of Ale, and can even name the four founding members (Michael Hardman, Graham Lees, Jim Makin and Bill Mellor). They were protesting against the dominance of the then 'Big Six' (Allied Breweries, Bass Charrington, Courage, Scottish & Newcastle, Whitbread and Watneys) and what they regarded as their high-handed, dismissive view of great British brewing traditions. The focus of CAMRA's ire was bland, artificially carbonated keg beer – parodied as 'Grotney's' in Bill Tidy's Keg Buster cartoon strip – and the increasingly popular, newfangled lagers, which were threatening the very existence of unpasteurised, unfiltered 'real' ale. Today, CAMRA has 125,000 members, and Grotney's is a humorous relic of a bygone era.

The line to take with CAMRA is that they have done – and continue to do – a sterling job, though there has been a danger of freeze-framing the definition of the 'perfect pint' in 1971 (when CAMRA was founded) when, in fact, there was still much room for improvement. Over the course of two world wars, a scarcity of brewing materials and the need for a sober workforce in Britain's munitions factories had led to a serious dilution of the classic ale styles, with many becoming pale, emasculated imitations of their former selves. But you can suggest that today's microbrewers are taking the British beer revolution to the next stage by putting back some balls and diversity. They are setting their sights well above ordinary bitter, and here are a few of your favourites: dark, viscous Old Engine Oil porter (6%) from the Harviestoun Brewery in Alva, Scotland; tangerine-tinged Halcyon Imperial IPA (7.4%) from the Thornbridge Brewery in Derbyshire; and Paradox Smokehead Oak-Aged Imperial Stout (10%), a burly yet sweetish Scottish stout, matured in a variety of ex-whisky casks by BrewDog. Refer also to the Meantime Brewing Company in Greenwich, which is drawing on London's legacy of stouts and porters, pale ales and IPAs to build a portfolio of anything-but-boring beers. Meantime is also a member of the London Brewers' Alliance, formed in 2010 'to unite those who make local beer with those that love it'. It seems not so long ago that the number of London breweries had dwindled to just two, Fuller's and Young's, but this new alliance has 14 brewery members (including Fuller's).

BREWING ABROAD

The craft brewing revolution has taken off, as anyone could have predicted, in countries with established beer-drinking cultures like Belgium, Denmark, Canada, Australia, New Zealand and even Japan. But kudos will be yours for knowing that Italy, the world's largest wine producer, is suddenly at the sharp end of zymology (the science of fermenting beer). It's not so surprising when you think about it, seeing as Italy is the birthplace of the international Slow Food movement, which is dedicated to protecting heritage and tradition in food and drink.

Arty, crafty Italian brewers leave the mass market to the big boys, aiming their complex, food-friendly beers at the restaurant trade instead, where they are competing directly with wine. Presentation, therefore, is extremely important, which is why Italian craft beers have a reputation for fancy-schmancy, cork-topped bottles and eye-catching glassware that would definitely look out of place with bangers and mash in Burton upon Trent. Italy's boutique *birrifici* (breweries) make the full range of beer styles, but draw most inspiration from Belgium with its pouring rituals and elaborately branded glassware for each and every beer.

Rooted in a culture of local specialities, Italian craft brewers often source ingredients from artisan food producers to season their beers. Highly innovative beers are flavoured with the likes of basil, sage, cardamom, peach and watermelon, but Italian brewers also seem to have a thing for chestnuts, which are the most commonly used flavouring ingredient. Possessing this knowledge, you would not be phased by a bottle of Torbata smoked ale (8.7%), flavoured with chestnut honey and orange peel, from the eccentrically named Almond '22 microbrewery in Abruzzo.

Experimentation is key in Italian craft brewing, with many maturing their beers in ex-whisky, wine and cognac barrels. But the latest trend, with which you are, of course, familiar, is the deliberate oxidation of high-strength ales so they take on sherry-like qualities. Usually, these are bottled without carbonation, to be sipped appreciatively, perhaps with a rock-hard parmesan or plate of bresaola.

Weird and wonderful ingredients aside, the most surprising thing about the Italian beer revolution is the speed with which it has happened. It started in the early 1990s, predominantly in the gastro-oriented north of the country, and there are already some 300 craft birrificios throwing a veritable bunga bunga beer party. Italian breweries to name-drop include Baladin, Musso, Grado Plato and Lambrate.

BACK IN THE USA

Back across the pond the inevitable has happened, and let's hope it's a forerunner of events elsewhere. The craft brewing movement has become so damn successful, and some of the protagonists so large, that in 2011 the Brewers Association had to revise its definition of 'craft' brewers. They must still be – relatively – small, independent and traditional but the cap on production has been raised from two million to six million barrels per year. You, of course, are too seasoned a pro to be taken in by romantic notions of mustachioed, aproned artisans stirring bubbling cauldrons, being aware that most craft brewers use state-of-the-art, computerised equipment. It seems appropriate, however, that the largest of them all, the Boston Beer Company, will always be associated with revolution, as several of its beers bear the name of Samuel Adams, signatory of the American Declaration of Independence. How fitting.

MISCEL-ALE-NEOUS

STEAM BEER

Steam beer is an ale/lager love child made with lager yeast but fermented at warm temperatures usually associated with ale brewing. As a result, this hybrid beer combines the malty fruitiness of ale with the crisp cleanness of lager – rather like German alt and kölsch beers, you might add. Also known as 'California Common', this product of rough-and-ready, frontier brewing techniques was the blue-collar beer of West Coast USA in the late nineteenth century. In its heyday steam beer was synonymous with San Francisco where, at the height of its popularity, there were some 25 steaming breweries. The style waned in popularity, perhaps partly due to its blue-collar image, until eventually only San Francisco's Anchor Brewing Company remained. By the mid-1960s even this last bastion of steam beer stood on the verge of bankruptcy, at which point, as previously mentioned, it was bought by 'Fritz' Maytag, a young student and heir to a successful washing machine company. There are echoes of the Pierre Celis/Hoegaarden story (*see* Belgian witbier, page 100), where a fan of a particular beer single-handedly revives a disappearing style; the difference being that Maytag thought to trademark the 'steam beer' name in 1981. Thus, steam beer is now a one-man brew, made only by Anchor Brewing in San Francisco. It's worth casually commenting that Maytag's rescue of the company is widely regarded as the catalyst that sparked the American craft beer movement.

'If you guys are going to be throwing beer bottles at us, at least make sure they're full.'

Dave Mustaine, Megadeth

So why is it called steam beer? That's a good question. Steam beer is fizzier than the average beer, but this won't score you many bluffing points. So how about – steam beer undergoes a second fermentation in the cask, increasing the pressure of carbon dioxide, which sounds like escaping steam when it is expelled. Of course, the amount of pressure depends on the level of 'kräusening' (a German term describing the addition of fermenting wort to induce fermentation). That should do it.

Anchor Steam Beer (4.9%) is an amber-coloured brew with strong carbonation and a creamy head. It's fruity and refreshing with a hint of caramel and a clean, dry finish. A bit like a cross between lager and ale, in fact.

ADELAIDE SPARKLING ALE

This iconic Aussie beer, also known as 'Australian pale ale', sticks out of the indigenous lager landscape as conspicuously as Ayers Rock (aka 'Uluru') at sunset. Like San Francisco's steam beer, Adelaide sparkling ale has come to be synonymous with one producer and one city; in this case, Coopers Brewery of Adelaide. Unlike its Californian counterpart, however, this is not a lager/ale hybrid but a straight-up top-fermented ale. It also happens to be unfiltered, unpasteurised and bottle-conditioned. As if this doesn't make it unusual enough in dyed-in-the-wool Lagerland, Coopers Sparkling Ale (5.8%) is cloudy when poured. Comment on its hefeweizen-like haziness as it swirls and settles in your glass (*see* German weissbier). This haziness comes from the yeast sediment produced by a secondary fermentation in bottle, which also contributes to the carbonation of this famously fizzy beer. Coopers Sparkling Ale is often described as tasting 'wheaty', 'grainy' and 'bready'. In other words, it tastes primarily of its yeast, but with a fruity undercurrent seasoned with Pride of Ringwood hops from Tasmania. First brewed by Thomas Cooper in 1862, this cultish ale is made by the largest, and one of the few, independent family brewers in Australia, now employing its sixth generation.

CHOCOLATE BEER

Usually, chocolate beers such as Brooklyn Black Chocolate Stout (with a whopping 10% ABV) derive their unique 'chocolateness' from a blend of dark-roasted 'chocolate malts', which are roasted just-so until they acquire natural mocha-like flavours. Increasingly, however, brewers are upping the ante by supplementing these chocolate malts with real chunks of chocolate or chocolate essence. Young's Double Chocolate Stout (5.2%) and Meantime Chocolate Porter (6.5%), for example, both add real chocolate. Obviously, most chocolate beers are souped-up stouts and porters.

Should anyone give you a hard time for drinking chocolate beer, point out that most of them taste of bitter, dark chocolate (as opposed to Terry's All Gold) with a pleasingly dry finish. Also mention that eighteenth-century Mexicans drank a cocoa-based brew, not unlike chocolate beer.

CHAMPAGNE BEER

Champagne beer, sometimes referred to as 'Bière Brut', is one of the more recent brewing trends, with which you are, of course, perfectly au fait. It is only quite recently that Belgian brewers have mastered the notoriously temperamental Champagne yeast, prompting a trend for light, dry, fizzy beers in the image of Champagne.

One of the better-known brands, Kasteel Cru (5.2%), is simply lager made with Champagne yeast. Deus Brut des Flandres, on the other hand, actually mimics the *méthode champenoise,* the method by which Champagne is made. It's matured with Champagne yeast for nine months in cool caves before *remuage* and *dégorgement.* After secondary fermentation has taken place, the bottle is gradually twisted and inverted over a period of time until the yeast sediment gathers in the upside-down neck (this is the *remuage* bit). *Dégorgement* is the process by which the bottleneck is frozen and the pellet of yeast is expelled. All this palaver is reflected in Champagne-style prices, but at least Deus Brut, for example, has a (nearly) Champagne strength of 11.5%. It comes in a Champagne-style bottle, complete with wired cork, and is popular, apparently, with the ladies.

GAY BEER

And finally, as they say on the evening news, gay beer from Mexico. Purple Hand Beer and Salamandra are marketed exclusively to the lesbian, gay, bisexual and transgender community (LGBT), and they come with detachable labels for the drinker to wear with pride. There is nothing inherently gay about the beers, which are infused with honey. Honey, of course, is made by single-sex communities, lauded over by domineering queens.

'You gotta get rid of all that macho crap that they [men] pick up from beer commercials.'

Roseanne Barr

THE BEER BEHEMOTHS

Your effortless barroom banter could cause insecurity among less 'knowledgeable' beer drinkers, who might accuse you of having wilfully obscure tastes. Modestly point out that anyone would have developed a similar penchant for esoteric farmhouse ales, if they'd spent as much time in northern France as you have. And, besides, who – outside China – has ever heard of Snow, which happens to be the bestselling beer brand in the world?

Broadly speaking, the major global beer brands are losing ground in the established Western markets in the USA and Europe due to the ongoing recession and the slow but steady rise of regional and craft brewing. Consequently, they find themselves jockeying for position in up-and-coming markets such as Brazil, Russia, India and China (the so-called BRIC countries), while the industry continues to consolidate into a dwindling number of planet-sized conglomerates.

For bluffing purposes you need concern yourself with the twin leviathans of AB InBev and SABMiller, respectively the world's largest and second-largest brewing companies. AB InBev was created in 2008, the result of a hostile $52 billion takeover of US brewer Anheuser-Busch by the Belgian company InBev, based in Leuven in the Flemish region of Belgium. Of course you've heard of it. At the time of the merger, the companies had annual sales of $36.4 billion, accounting for about one-quarter of the global beer market. That's a lot of beer. The company's major brands are Budweiser, Beck's and Stella Artois.

In 2002, South African Breweries (SAB) purchased the American Miller Brewing Company to form SABMiller, with its head office in London. In 2008, SABMiller joined forces with Molson Coors to create a US distribution joint venture called Miller Coors, to improve competitiveness with AB InBev in this vital market.

Reading any 'serious' beer book (apart from this one, obviously), you would have no idea that the world's top 10 beer brands even existed. They are barely mentioned in zymurgical tomes, and this can only be because they are not deemed worthy of critical appraisal; and this is probably due to the broad consensus that, by and large, these mass-produced brands taste pretty much the same. There are no genuine ales among the top 10. There isn't 'a hoppy one', 'a strong one' or 'a fruity one'. They are all light, pale, easy-drinking lagers with no perceptible hop bitterness. They are all clean, crisp and dry, appealing to squillions by virtue of their inoffensiveness.

In fairness, these beers aren't designed for sipping and savouring or for quiet contemplation. They're built for chugging, as chilled as possible. And, as you are aware, the colder a beer is, the less danger there is of any 'flavour' creeping through. Most of these top-10 brands 'deliver' refreshment in much the same way as a brand of chewing gum might. Essentially, the target audience is buying into carefully nurtured brand concepts, reinforced by iconic packaging and catchy slogans. Thus, Miller Lite has a 'refreshingly drinkable taste' and Corona Extra manages, somehow, to achieve 'the unparalleled flavour of relaxation'. All the above said, there is a definite place for this sort of beer. Not only do vast numbers of happy drinkers love it, but – rather like franchised fried chicken outlets – they are a guilty secret which many 'serious' beer lovers find it difficult to admit to. And then there's the temperature. Imagine the following scene: you're in a sweltering beach bar in the tropics, and you're offered a frosted bottle of Chug Ice Lite, or a pint of Old Gruntfuttlecock? Be honest – what's your poison?

For ease of reference, here is a snapshot of the world's top 10 beer brands as this guide went to press. Unfortunately, we cannot guarantee that adopting any of these brands will put a blonde on each arm as you jet-ski into the horizon to a soft-rock soundtrack. But you never know.

SNOW (50.8M* BARRELS; SABMILLER)

In 2011 the Chinese chugged 16.5 billion pints of Snow, which has overtaken Bud Light for the global number-one spot. Its performance is hardly surprising – it is the most popular brand in the world's biggest beer market, which

* 2011 volumes.

is growing by about 5% per annum. It is said that if all Chinese beer drinkers shook their bottles and opened them simultaneously, the whole world would be ankle-deep in Snow.

BUD LIGHT (45.4M BARRELS; AB INBEV)

Bud Light is America's bestselling beer, and still a global powerhouse. Launched in 1982, it came relatively late to the US light beer market, but now accounts for about half the sales in this enormous category. You might not be too surprised to learn that calorie-conscious Americans have made light beer (lower-calorie beer) the largest sector by far in the US beer market. Bud Light Lime, essentially the same drink with a splash of lime, was introduced by Bud Light in 2008. It was joined in 2012 by something called 'Lime-a-Rita', an 8% ABV margarita-flavoured 'malt beverage'. The most recent addition to the Bud Light range of brands is the alarming-sounding 'Strawber-Rita', which apparently 'blends the refreshment of Bud Light Lime with the taste of an authentic strawberry margarita'. If you find yourself despairing at the future of the brewing industry, rest assured that these concoctions are not actually beers. They are alcopops.

BUDWEISER (38.7M BARRELS; AB INBEV)

'The king of beers' was introduced in 1876 when Adolphus Busch set out to create America's first truly national beer brand. Today, Budweiser is the only full-calorie option among America's top five beers (always ask for 'full-fat' if you want to prove your drinking credentials). It is not to be confused with Budweiser Budvar from the Czech Republic. With up to 30% rice in the grist (the mix of grains and cereals comprising the mash), Budweiser likes to trumpet its 'traditional beechwood ageing process'. While beechwood chips are used in the maturation tank, they make little to no flavour contribution as they are boiled for several hours beforehand. Their purpose it to increase the surface area at the bottom of the tank, allowing more yeast cells to come into contact with the developing beer. This functions as a filter to speed up the removal of unwanted diacetyl (butterscotch) and acetaldehyde (green apple) flavours, obviously. Tell that to a barman, and he'll probably call for security.

CORONA EXTRA (30.4M BARRELS; AB INBEV)

Mexico's leading brewer Grupo Modelo, producer of Corona Extra, was swallowed whole by AB InBev in 2012, increasing the global brewer's access to the Mexican beer market, which is currently growing by about 3% a year. Corona Extra is Mexico's bestselling beer and the number-one imported beer in the USA and Canada. It is served in more than 150 countries, frequently with a wedge of lime in the neck of the bottle, a practice that the Mexicans are mystified by and happy to leave to the tourists. Examine Corona's distinctive clear glass bottle and mutter darkly about how the contents are susceptible to 'lightstrike' (when sunlight reacts with hop resins creating 'skunky' flavours). Brown glass, obviously, would have been better. Corona's marketing department would reply, however, 'when you use only the finest ingredients, you've got nothing to hide.' Because, you see, 'Corona is more than just a beer. It represents a philosophy of living in the moment that has been embraced around the world.'

SKOL (29.5M BARRELS; CARLSBERG BREWERIES)

In the late 1980s, Skol was the UK's biggest-selling beer, but today it is a low-price commodity lager that would not trouble the top 20. In the UK it's even been reduced to a mere 2.8% ABV, taking advantage of a new low-alcohol tax band. Meanwhile, Skol lager with a far more respectable 4.7% ABV is the bestselling beer in Brazil, where it is considered as Brazilian as bikini waxing and beach soccer. You can explain this schizophrenic brand thus: in 1964 Allied Breweries (UK), Labatt (Canada), Pripps-Bryggerierna (Sweden) and Unibra (Belgium) formed a new company called Skol International. Its aim was to create a global beer brand that could be licensed, manufactured and marketed throughout the world. Today, due to brewery mergers and takeovers far too convoluted to go into here, the Skol brand is owned by Carlsberg in Europe and Asia, by AB InBev in South America, and by Unibra in Africa. It's available in more than 80 countries, but is particularly big in Brazil, the Congo and Malaysia.

HEINEKEN (26M BARRELS; HEINEKEN INTERNATIONAL)

What can we tell you? It's the Dutch lager that 'refreshes the parts other beers cannot reach'. Could this be why

James Bond was seen clutching a bottle of Heineken in Skyfall? Or was it the £28 million product-placement deal that persuaded him to forsake his traditional vodka martini? The next time you see the iconic green bottle with the red star, point out to anyone that will listen that the 'e's in 'Heineken' are tilted at an angle to make them look as if they are 'smiling', allegedly.

COORS LIGHT (18.2M BARRELS; MOLSON COORS)

'The coldest tasting beer in the world' was first brewed in Golden, Colorado in 1978, 'inspired by the mountains where it originated'. Cold is very important to Coors. 'Cold Coors Light is good,' we are told. 'Super cold Coors Light is better.' This is achieved through 'cold-activated' glassware featuring a mountain logo. 'When the mountains turn blue you know the beer in your glass is as cold as the Rockies,' apparently.

MILLER LITE (18M BARRELS; SABMILLER)

Launched in 1973 with its devil-may-care spelling, Miller Lite was the first nationally available light beer in the USA. Not to be outdone by Coors's 'cold-activated' glasses, Miller Lite has a 'taste activator' glass with a laser-etched Miller Lite logo on the bottom; basically, it's nucleated to produce a constant stream of bubbles. Also worthy of note is the brand's Vortex bottle: '…with specially designed grooves inside the neck, the Vortex bottle lets the great taste flow right out.' Removing the cap has much the same effect.

BRAHMA (17.4M BARRELS; AB INBEV)

Originally made by the Companhia Cervejaria Brahma in 1888, Brahma beer is now owned by AB InBev, which has big plans to take the brand global. For years it was sold in Brazil as 'The number one beer', though it has had to quietly drop this slogan since being overtaken by Skol. What attracted AB InBev to Brahma? Was it the taste of the beer? 'First and foremost it was the emotional context,' said a company spokesman. 'The culture was more important in terms of filling a positioning that we had identified on a global basis. The emotional context of Brahma, at the heart and soul of this incredible country called Brazil, was the single most important factor.' It's intended to convey the idea of 'living with effortless flair' (or 'living with effortless flatulence', as one unkind commentator put it).

ASAHI SUPER DRY (12.3M BARRELS; ASAHI)

Asahi Super Dry was launched in 1987 as Japan's first 'karakuchi' (dry) beer. Specifically designed to complement food, it quickly became the most popular beer in the massive Japanese beer market. It's available in over 50 countries, having carved a niche for itself in sushi and noodle bars in Europe. Bluffers take note: it is perfectly acceptable to extol the crisp, dry virtues of Asahi beer, as many 'serious' beer writers do. Perhaps it is because of the brand's culinary aspirations, or because it gains credence through association with Asahi Black (dark lager) and Asahi Stout.

There's no point in pretending that you know everything about beer – nobody does – but if you've got this far and you've absorbed at least a modicum of the information and advice contained within these pages, then you will almost certainly know more than 99% of the rest of the human race about what beer is, how it is made, where it is made, how it is served, and how it is drunk.

What you now do with this information is up to you, but here's a suggestion: be confident about your newfound knowledge, see how far it takes you, but above all have fun using it. You are now a bona fide expert in the art of bluffing about one of the world's oldest and most deservedly popular drinks. And bear in mind that the only bluffing skill you really need to master is to choose your moment carefully and keep your mouth shut the rest of the time. That's easy enough to do when it's full of a delicately balanced and aromatic composite of barley, yeast, water and hops.

Nunc est bibendum! ('Now let's drink!')

Think you're ready for the pub with your knowledge of beer? Test it first with our quiz at bluffers.com.

GLOSSARY

ABV (Alcohol By Volume) The percentage of your beer that is pure alcohol, and therefore the best indicator of how many you can drink before picking a fight with the fruit machine. Multiply ABV by 0.796 for ABW (Alcohol By Weight).

Adjuncts Sources of fermentable sugar other than malted barley, including alternative grains, fruits and syrups.

Ale *See* 'top-fermented'.

Alpha acid The bittering compound in hops, contributing most of beer's bitterness.

Barrel The most common unit of measurement for beer production. A British barrel is 163.65 litres (36 imperial gallons), while a US barrel is 117.34 litres (31 US gallons). Derive further bluffing from firkins (9 imperial gallons), kilderkins (18 gallons), hogsheads (54 gallons), puncheons (72 gallons) and butts (108 gallons, the largest and now rarely used).

Bottle-conditioned Beer that is conditioned (i.e., matured and finished) in a bottle. A little sugar and yeast are added to provoke a further fermentation in the bottle, which adds complexity and sometimes strength. A layer of sediment (dead yeast) in the base of the bottle is a telltale sign of bottle-conditioning.

Bottom-fermented Lager-style beer resulting from cold fermentation by yeast of the Saccharomyces uvarum family. Lager yeasts operate best in cool conditions where they sink to the bottom of the tank, slowly nibbling away at the sugars for up to two weeks, resulting in a less sweet, more refreshing beer. *Lager* means 'to store' in German, reflecting the fact that lagers, ideally, should be given a long, cool conditioning period. Some prefer the term 'cold-fermented' to 'bottom-fermented' but it's nowhere near as funny-sounding.

Brettanomyces A strain of wild yeast that gives a sour finish to beer, sometimes with farmyardy, horse blanket flavours. Desirable in lambic beers, sour brown and red Flanders ales and some wheat beers, stouts and porters. Should you detect any of these sharp, rustic qualities in your beer, attribute it to 'a touch of Brett'.

Cask-conditioned Describes beers, neither filtered nor pasteurised, that undergo a secondary fermentation in the barrel, usually at the point of sale in a pub's cellar. The additional fermentation adds strength and complexity. Cask-conditioned beer is also referred to as 'real ale', a term first coined in the 1970s by CAMRA (Campaign for Real Ale).

Craft beer When craft brewing took off in the USA in the 1980s, 'craft beer' meant interesting, artisanal beer made on a small scale. But now that some 'craft' brewers produce hundreds of thousands of barrels, this definition is shifting away from the 'small' part and focusing on the 'interesting' bit. It now describes any beer that can be seen as a backlash against the mega-brands. Craft brewing is the opposite of 'industrial brewing'.

Double Adjective originally slapped in front of certain American IPAs to denote a strong and massively hopped, and therefore very bitter, style. Now 'Double' is increasingly used to indicate a stronger, fuller-bodied version of any beer style. *See* also 'Imperial'.

Dry hopping The practice of adding hops to beer during its conditioning period for additional hop flavour and aroma.

Extreme beer A term favoured by surf dudes and Pepsi Max drinkers to describe high-strength, unusual, 'out there' beers; an 8%, wild-fermented, barrel-aged, chestnut-flavoured beer, for example. The antithesis of 'lawnmower lager'.

Filtration The removal of unwanted particles from beer. Unfortunately, flavour can also be removed by over-zealous filtration.

Grist The mix of grains that goes into the mash.

Gruit Traditionally a mixture of dried herbs and spices, used to flavour beers, before the widespread adoption of hops. These days 'gruit' is sometimes used to describe any beer made entirely without hops.

High-gravity brewing A production method commonly used in industrial brewing whereby beer is fermented to a high percentage of alcohol then reduced with water to the desired strength just before packaging.

Imperial Originally used to denote a strong and intensely flavoured style of stout shipped from England to the Imperial Russian court in the eighteenth and nineteenth centuries. Like the term 'double', it is now haphazardly used to describe an unusually strong version of any beer style.

Industrial brewing A derogatory term to describe the production of beer on a massive scale by multinational companies, often using 'high-gravity brewing'. But with beer, just like everything else in life, big doesn't automatically mean bad.

International Bittering Units (IBU) An international scale for expressing the level of alpha acids (hop bitterness) in beer. An IBU rating is achieved via a complex calculation based on the weight of hops, alpha acids, wort and alcohol. One IBU is equivalent to one milligram of alpha acid per litre of beer. A heavily hopped double IPA might have 65+ IBU, while a feeble lawnmower lager might contain just 10.

IPA (India Pale Ale) A heavily hopped style of pale ale developed in England in the nineteenth century, using the antibacterial, preservative qualities of hops to help the beer withstand the gruelling voyage to India. The American craft brewing movement has taken this style to heart, competing to produce the most powerfully hopped double IPAs.

Keg Metal container in which beer is stored under artificial pressure from carbon dioxide, or a mixed carbon dioxide and nitrogen system.

Lager *See* 'bottom-fermented'.

Lawnmower lager Uncomplicated, light-bodied lager fit only for chugging in the garden.

Lightstrike or sunstrike Ailment suffered by bottled beers when excessive exposure to light causes their hop oils to degrade, producing a vegetal, rubbery, wet-dog smell, sometimes described as 'skunky'. Brown glass is best for prevention, followed by green glass; clear glass is useless.

Liquor The name for hot water used in the 'mashing' process. Mere 'water' is something used to clean the brewery and hose down the tanks.

Malt Grains, usually barley, where germination (sprouting) has been encouraged by steeping in water. This provokes the production of starch, which is converted into fermentable sugars during the brewing process. Malted grains are dried, cured and toasted to varying degrees in a kiln, producing shades and flavours ranging from pale to dark-roasted.

Mash Porridge-like mixture of ground malted and unmalted grains (grist), sometimes with adjuncts to which liquor (hot water) is added to convert grain starch into fermentable sugars. The resulting sugary solution is called 'wort'.

Nitrokeg Type of beer stored under nitrogen in kegs. Nitrogen has smaller bubbles than carbon dioxide, creating smoother, creamier beer. Guinness is the most famous nitrokeg beer.

Original gravity (OG) Measurement of the fermentable sugars in wort, relative to the density of water, prior to fermentation. This gives brewers a good indication of the eventual alcoholic strength of a beer. With water density given a base value of 1.000, OG is usually expressed as a four-digit number without the decimal point. Thus, 1.050 OG is expressed as 1050. Simple.

Pasteurisation A means of killing bacteria and stabilising beer by applying heat for a brief period of time. Sadly, it's detrimental to beer flavour.

Real ale *See* 'cask-conditioned'.

Session beer Any beer below 4% ABV, intended for serial quaffing.

Top-fermented Ale-style beer resulting from warm fermentation by yeast of the Saccharomyces cerevisiae family, also referred to as 'warm-fermented'. Ale yeasts rise to the top of the fermentation tank, gorging on sugars in a frenzy of foam, heat and fury, resulting in sweeter, rounder and fruitier styles, as compared with lager.

Wort Sugar-rich liquid produced by mashing, i.e., mixing malted grains with hot water. Wort is boiled with hops then cooled before fermentation.

WYBMABIITY A sign sometimes seen behind bars. The letters stand for 'Will You Buy Me A Beer If I Tell You?' Don't fall for this old chestnut.

Yeast A microscopic, single-cell fungus that is the magic ingredient in fermentation, consuming sugar and producing alcohol and carbon dioxide (fizz).

Zymurgy The science of brewing beer.

BLUFFING NOTES

Bluffing Notes

Bluffing Notes

Bluffing Notes

Bluffing Notes

Bluffing Notes

NEW EDITIONS

Hold your own in any situation with these new and forthcoming Bluffer's Guides®.

BOND
CARS
CHOCOLATE
CRICKET
DOGS
ETIQUETTE
FOOD
FOOTBALL
GOLF
HIKING
INSIDER HOLLYWOOD
JAZZ
MANAGEMENT

OPERA
POETRY
QUANTUM UNIVERSE
ROCK MUSIC
RUGBY
SEX
SKIING
SURFING
TENNIS
UNIVERSITY
WINE
YOUR OWN BUSINESS

BLUFFERS.COM
@BLUFFERSGUIDE